What others are saying about *From the Ground Up*:

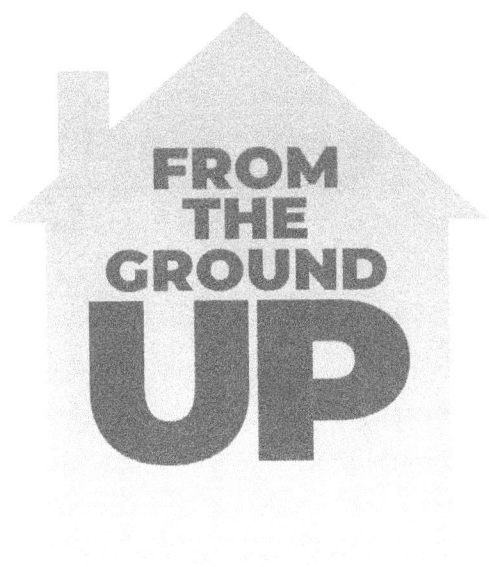

FROM
THE
GROUND
UP

FROM THE GROUND UP

HOW TWO MILLENNIAL HIGH SCHOOL SWEETHEARTS CREATED A MULTIMILLION-DOLLAR REAL ESTATE INVESTMENT PORTFOLIO FROM SCRATCH—AND YOU CAN TOO

DR. CÉLINE H. HIGGINS EVANS
AND CHRISTOPHER S. EVANS

The information presented herein represents the view of the authors as of the date of publication. This book is presented for informational purposes only. Neither the authors nor the publisher is engaged in rendering legal, investment, or other professional advice. If legal advice or other expert assistance is required, the services of a competent professional should be sought.

ISBN (paperback) 979-8-9880421-0-5
ISBN (ebook) 979-8-9880421-1-2
ISBN (audiobook) 979-8-9880421-2-9

Published by Haruka Scott Holdings, LLC, www.hshbrands.com/ FromTheGroundUp

Contact the authors at info@hshbrands.com

For James, Scarlett, and Amélie Clare

CONTENTS

INTRODUCTION

"How'd you build wealth with real
estate? I wish I could do that."

That's what people ask us all the time. What works for us might work for you—or not. This book gives you the guidance we wish we had had while building our real estate portfolio. Of course, we don't have all the answers for everyone, but we welcome you to look at our success story and see what you can do to build wealth using real estate.

This is not another get-rich-quick how-to book. Building wealth takes time and expertise. What are you willing to do to retire early? Is your money working for you or for the bank?

Many people believe that real estate is a fundamental part of investing for their futures. In fact, owning the hard asset of real estate can give multiple financial benefits that can't always be found just through Wall Street investments.

The investor building a real estate portfolio must figure out how to obtain the real estate assets, when to do so, and what kind to select. They must create their own team of professionals that includes financial advisors, CPAs, lawyers, insurance agents, and, of course, real estate agents.

In this book, we detail how we, two millennial high school sweethearts, created a multimillion-dollar real estate portfolio from scratch by our mid-30s over 14 years. Although our story tells of our experiences through the eyes of a millennial couple, the foundations of our portfolio teach valuable knowledge about how you can create your own investment portfolio over time—through a strong or weak real estate market.

Our portfolio has a projected retirement age in our early 50s with monthly passive income (also known as "mailbox money"). Our net worth from the portfolio is respectable, and more than the minimum for our projected retirement age.

We provide an outline with steps to get started on your own real estate portfolio in the last chapter of this book. A custom *Evans Report for Real Estate Planning* is also described at the end and portfolio planning service is available.

You can do this too!

CHAPTER 1

OPPOSITES ATTRACT

We (Céline and Chris) met when we were 14 and 15 years old. Our backgrounds couldn't have been any more different.

Chris comes from a blue-collar family from Berkley, Massachusetts, which is a small agricultural town about halfway between Cape Cod and Providence, Rhode Island. It is the typical small town in the northern United States.

After serving in the US Air Force, his father started his career in telecom, where he worked himself up from a cable installer to a national support engineer for corporate communication systems. His mother was a stay-at-home mom when Chris was young, but she would also work nights as a manager for the local newspaper as Chris got older.

His family moved to Georgia while he was in grade school, and he went on to graduate from the public school system in suburban Atlanta. He is the first from his family to graduate from a university.

Céline is from a military family with a long history of service in almost every generation, starting with the Revolutionary War. She was born in Atlanta, Georgia, and grew up in the north metro Atlanta area suburbs. Her half-Japanese and half-American dual-citizenship parents were born and raised in Japan on American bases. They had moved to the United States in the 1970s after her father was drafted into the US Army during the Vietnam War.

Her father and mother were entrepreneurs who coordinated Japanese TV shows and movies for Japanese TV networks. Later, her parents opened their own non-franchise real estate brokerage in Marietta, Georgia, called Sellect Realty.

We met each other in our high school years, but attended different schools in the same county. We were engaged to be married at 19 after dating for two years. Not all early commitments are mistakes. Some people know when they have met the right partner, because here we are more than 20 years and three amazing children later.

We decided to attend the University of Georgia for our undergraduate degrees because it allowed us to pursue different interests while being together. Céline studied biology at the Franklin College of Arts and Sciences while Chris studied political science at the School of Public & International Affairs.

Tuition was rising rapidly during this time, and we had decided to take advantage of the HOPE Scholarship that Georgia offers its residents. We could not in good conscience *not* take advantage of such an opportunity to have our undergraduate tuition paid for. The United States did not, and still does not, have a free or discounted tuition model like the developed countries of Norway, Finland, Germany, France, Denmark, and Sweden.

Neither of us had parents who had saved much at all to help us pay for higher education tuition or living expenses. We were essentially on our own. We are forever thankful to the State of Georgia for providing this opportunity without subjecting us to a school debt that would have been difficult to pay back in our working years. We do not discount our help from the state in this early stage of our lives.

Chris developed a deeper love of reading while in college. He chose to read books such as *Rich Dad Poor Dad* by Robert Kiyosaki and *The Millionaire Next Door* by Thomas J. Stanley and William Danko while working part-time at a bank during the week. He was so inspired by these books that he quickly applied to switch his major and was accepted into the finance program in UGA's Terry College of Business. The wisdom in these books also ignited a spark of interest in real estate that was yet to be fully realized.

Looking back, we have concluded that we were somewhat misled by what seemed to be the middle-class mantra at the time—that a college degree is the ticket to financial stability and freedom. We can remember our parents harping on us to attend because they thought that college was the pathway to the best future for us. Without a college degree, we wouldn't have the "stamp of approval" in being a hirable adult.

We thought our lives after our high school years would look something like this:

Go to college. Get a job. Make a family (maybe?). Retire.

Now, we have a different view of the value of an undergraduate college degree. We no longer blindly believe that this education is a sure path to guaranteed success and financial stability—not that there ever was an actual guarantee.

An article published by *Bloomberg News* in April 2022 reported that a quarter of US college graduates make less than $35,000 per year, or are at near-poverty levels. More than half the graduates do not work in their chosen field of study after they attain their degrees. The article said, "The average student loan debt increased 4.5% between 2020 and 2021, with public school graduates borrowing an average of $30,030 for a bachelor's degree . . . Out of the college grads surveyed, nearly half live paycheck to paycheck. Many reported putting off major financial milestones like buying a home or a car because they couldn't afford it, and 29% said they were uncertain that they'll be able to pay their rent or mortgage every month."

These numbers are hardly appealing when examined and stripped down to what a degree really amounts to.

Could this be the trend that makes a college degree equivalent to what a high school diploma was worth to employers merely half a century ago? Should people chain themselves to college debt for years to come in the prime of their lives when they could actively be building wealth and equity through investments?

We don't know with certainty what the right answers are to these questions. The monetary aspect of higher education is a significant commitment for returns that are not guaranteed.

Céline decided to pursue a doctorate in veterinary medicine during her sophomore year of undergraduate school. This degree would cost a considerable amount in tuition compared to the average yearly earnings for doctors. We reviewed alternative avenues to enter the career of veterinary medicine and did not make any decisions about attending quickly. Unfortunately, there was no way to become a licensed veterinarian without a degree in veterinary medicine from an accredited school in the US. She *had* to go if she wanted to practice veterinary medicine.

A decision was made that life should not always be about how much you make per year, but also about doing something you love. We could not imagine decades of work in a subject we are not passionate about. The graduate school tuition was still a large financial consideration, and we decided to only take out federal student loans to pay for it. The main reason we didn't take any private loans is because income-based repayment plans were available for the federal student loans only.

There was also much uncertainty that she would even be accepted to veterinary school because of the limited number of accredited veterinary schools in the United States and seats available to applicants each year. Yet, she was determined and was accepted into not only one but two veterinary schools the first year she applied in 2008 for the Class of 2012: University of Georgia in Athens, Georgia, and Auburn University in Auburn, Alabama.

She chose to go to her in-state school to keep tuition costs at a minimum. Sadly, there were not many scholarships in the veterinary field, and working a side job while attending classes was absolutely not possible. There was just too much material to learn, and the time obligation to attend the school's classes did not leave a student any time to do anything other than study.

(Most students in her class graduated with a substantial amount of student debt—over $150,000. This is before student loan interest that would accrue in the following years. There were only two students Céline knew of, siblings, who were fortunate enough to graduate without owing a balance. Their father had paid for it all.)

Another decision we needed to make was housing. Athens, Georgia, is a classic, rural college town more than 70 miles away from where her parents lived in Marietta. Staying with them during these years to save money was not physically possible. It would take 1½ hours minimum of driving through Atlanta traffic each way, before and after classes. If you have ever been to Atlanta and experienced the traffic, you know it can cause large, unexpected delays that can throw your entire day off schedule. No thank you. We had no choice but to live in Athens.

As a couple we decided an important goal was to have a real estate portfolio as part of our investment strategy. Chris had been briefly introduced to real estate investing through the books he had read in his sophomore year of undergraduate school (notably, as mentioned, *Rich Dad Poor Dad* and *The Millionaire Next Door*, among others).

The logical conclusion was to purchase a home in Athens close to the College of Veterinary Medicine that Céline was to attend. Before this, we had been renting a small, affordable apartment together as an engaged couple for a year. We knew that we were both committing to four more years in the same college town for her doctorate degree, and no longer wanted to pay the apartment complex to pay off their commercial mortgage.

We were in a sense paying 100% interest to a landlord for a property to rent. Having a mortgage of our own was a much better option for our future in our books.

Céline's parents had opened their own real estate brokerage a year earlier. They named it Sellect Realty. They educated us on the differences between the types of properties for sale and what each meant for our futures. They were supportive of our desire to become homeowners at such an early age. This support was appreciated because we were the typical first-time homebuyer—scared of the unknown and intimidated by the process we had never undertaken before.

The first step we took toward our purchase was deciding what to look for. We created a must-have list of the most important points the property should have based on our financial goals and budget. And then we discuss why we chose these features.

Our Must-Have List
- Fee simple. Well maintained.
- Almost no front yard and backyard to keep lawn care needs at a minimum.
- Reasonable homeowners' association costs (if there is an HOA).
- Ability to rent the property to a tenant in the future.
- Reasonable property taxes.
- Two sinks in the master bathroom.

Fee simple: A legal definition of a freehold estate in land. The property is owned by the tenant without limitations or conditions—the highest form of ownership of a property. A common example is a single-family residential house that the owner may sell, lease, or pass on to beneficiaries.

Well maintained: This is important because of time and, of course, cost. We did not have time to spare in fixing small problems around the house on an ongoing basis while we lived there. Our time needed to be spent actively working and studying. Every repair also adds up in cost. A small fix here and there could set us back a few hundred dollars when we could be using the money to pay for a portion of the monthly mortgage.

Almost no front yard and backyard: This is important for the same reason we wanted a property that was well maintained. We did not have the time to spend on upkeep of the yard, nor did we have money to spare in hiring a lawn maintenance crew to do it for us. A minimal yard was all we could handle.

Why HOA costs need to be reasonable: Costs for a homeowners' association can quickly add up. Fees are commonly a monthly payment, and neighborhoods often have mandatory membership for the residents. Sometimes, there are even initiation fees on top of regular monthly fees. These fees can always change, so we needed to be careful.

We also wanted to make sure we were getting a value for what was included in the fees. We knew we would be responsible for paying for what wasn't covered. That's an added cost you can't forget to consider.

Why the ability to rent the property after: Per the ownership structure and HOA covenants, we could eventually rent the property to a tenant after Céline graduated from the College of Veterinary Medicine. The ability to rent to a tenant after was one of the most important items on the list to us.

We were set on incorporating real estate as part of our investment portfolio due to Chris's knowledge of finance and what he had studied at the Terry College of Business. We did not want to sell a property that we had already started to pay for, and challenged ourselves to keep the home until it was paid off, or could be used toward better real estate investments.

Renters would pay the mortgage off for us after we moved out. Every repair we made to the property would be considered "an investment" in the upkeep of our assets. There are also benefits we wanted to take advantage of. Many tax benefits are available only when you own an investment property.

Two sinks: This item is a completely selfish request based on nothing other than the fact that it was something both of us wanted. Why the heck not? We didn't want to bump into each other every morning while trying to brush our teeth.

We settled on a townhouse, close to the Broad River, that had been recently renovated and changed from a rental apartment complex into a fee simple complex. There was a home warranty, all-new appliances, HVAC, roof, and water heater included with the purchase. It had a tiny backyard that you could consider more of a shady patch of grass, and about 20 square feet of a front yard. The only thing it didn't have on our list was two sinks in the master bathroom. Oh well.

This property was a close enough match to our needs, although it wasn't Céline's dream home by any means (partly because it didn't have two sinks), and she never fell in love with the townhouse while she lived there. We had to remind ourselves throughout our stay that we bought the property for the utility of the house, not because it was adorable. Our preferences did not matter as much as the items on our must-have list.

We decided to finance this property with down payment assistance through the Georgia Dream Program and a 30-year conventional home loan. The down payment required for the loan was 5% of the purchase price. The Georgia Dream Program helps low-income, first-time home-buyers. This program required the down payment to be identified as a separate loan to be paid back in full over time. We were definitely considered low income as students. We had part-time jobs in undergraduate school and had never owned a home before.

There were so many hoops, caveats, and obstacles when it came to actually applying for the Georgia Dream Program that it was aptly nick-named the Georgia Nightmare Program. Nothing worth doing is easy, right? We slogged through the application process that was necessary for us to obtain the loan and, eventually, got it.

Our first home, a townhouse, near the university in Athens.

There are similar down payment assistance programs in other states across the US that are also available to first-time homebuyers. These programs change quite often and vary by state, so contact your licensed loan officer for the most current information.

These are the basic kinds of home loans that may be available to you to purchase residential property:

Conventional loan: A loan available for a primary, secondary, or investment property. Better credit scores, lower debt-to-income ratio, and a larger down payment amount is typically required than for other types of loans. This loan is not backed by the US government.

FHA loan: A loan only available for your primary residence for low-income to middle-income borrowers. This loan is backed by the Federal Housing Administration and requires mortgage insurance to be added to monthly payments. Lower credit scores, higher debt-to-income ratio, and lower down payment amounts are generally accepted as conditions for loan approval.

VA loan: A primary residence loan available from the US Department of Veterans Affairs. For US veterans, their surviving spouses, or active service members. The loan is not based on credit scores and offers 100% financing with no down payment and no mortgage insurance payments required, but a funding fee is usually charged to the borrower. Check with a loan officer to see if you qualify for a funding fee waiver.

USDA loan: A loan from the US Department of Agriculture to promote rural homeownership for single-family, detached houses that are bought as primary residences. This loan also has an option for 100% financing, but requires mortgage insurance and geographical restrictions. Income limits apply.

Cash: Often considered the king of financing. An attractive option for buyers as it does not require interest payments or a large amount for closing costs. No underwriting is required. Sellers like to accept this type of financing because it can take two weeks or less to close a contract. Do not confuse this financing with hard money loans, which are loans usually provided by nontraditional lenders.

Since there are so many ways money can be earned in real estate, it can be difficult to quantify monetary returns on a property down to the exact penny. Tax savings, the actual positive (or negative) cash flow, the equity growth, depreciation, and the asset appreciation from the market also need to be accounted for.

For the purposes of this book, we will only be comparing one property to another for simplicity's sake, while understanding that there are always other factors at play to consider.

CHAPTER 2

THE CRASH

The real estate market was still going strong when we signed the contract for our first house in the middle of 2008. While working to buy our first property, Chris was working a summer internship with Merrill Lynch to gain experience during his junior collegiate year.

The internship role was to support a team of senior wealth advisors by studying financial reports of companies in order to calculate their long-term values. He would then compare what these companies were trading for on Wall Street. If a company was trading for less than the calculated value, he would suggest to the wealth managers to recommend the stock, which they did often.

The internship was unpaid, and gasoline prices were over $5 a gallon. The commute by car to his internship was also over an hour total each day while we were staying with Céline's parents in Marietta for the summer.

The lack of pay from this time was a struggle, but the internship had fueled a passion for advising others. He was hooked, and knew he wanted to use this knowledge to help not only our family but others to plan for their future.

Chris was 21 years old, and Céline was 22 with our first home under contract and little income from Céline working over the summer. Then, the real estate crash hit.

Did this catastrophe matter to us with our pending home purchase? Yes and no. We had no way of knowing how the market would turn out, but we did know we would have to pay for a roof to live under through veterinary school. We might as well pay ourselves, right?

Remember, a goal of ours for this house was to keep it in our portfolio for a long time, not just for two or three years. Our ultimate goal was to pay it off in full from the rental income we would eventually receive from our tenants when we moved after graduation or to use the equity to purchase more real estate investments. We were in the long-term real estate portfolio camp, not the short-term.

With this said, there's also never a perfect time to buy a home. The real estate market is always shifting toward a buyer's market or a seller's market like a seesaw at the local park. People's lives are also constantly moving from one phase to another with obstacles, whether personal or related to work, that need to be overcome. Knowing what you can and can't do with the resources you have at the time is what sets many successful real estate investors apart from real estate investors who fail.

Our mortgage was reasonable because we had bought for utility, and the price we paid for the townhouse was modest. The monthly mortgage was well within our budget. We knew from our calculations before the crash that our mortgage could be paid with a part-time job's earnings or just Céline's student loan as part of her living expenses.

We decided not to panic and purchased the property. Again, we weren't intending to sell any time soon. Instead, we put our energy into learning how to be homeowners for the first time.

Our current real estate portfolio inventory (2008)

Fee simple townhouse as a primary residence.

We moved into our new home while Céline attended orientation week for veterinary school. We didn't hire movers or rent a moving truck because we were watching every penny we had. The move required multiple short trips with the aging mid-sized sedans we had bought with cash saved up just prior to our home purchase.

Sometimes, a little elbow grease is needed to get the job done and stay in budget. We were determined to stay out of unnecessary debt, which proved to be a good decision because we saw our home value begin a steady decline over the next few months to eventually be worth a fraction of what we paid for it. Ouch!

The Wharton School of the University of Pennsylvania published an article on the causes of the 2008 housing crisis. Of the main factors for the crash, these experts said this: "A primary mistake that fueled the housing bubble was the rush to lend money to home buyers without regard for their ability to repay . . . They also increased access to credit, both for those with low credit scores and middle-class homeowners who wanted to take out a second lien on their home or a home equity line of credit. In doing so, they created a lot of leverage in the system and introduced a lot more risk."

The Principle of Leverage

If a buyer borrows money to purchase a property and the home value declines, the buyer will have less, or even negative, equity. And this is where real estate started going off the rails in 2008. We explain.

Leverage is the use of borrowed money to purchase assets that are worth more than the borrowed amount.

This investment tactic is commonly used in real estate with home loans (mortgages). The return on the investment made must be more than debt servicing cost to be profitable.

Here we compare two hypothetical portfolios created with $200,000 in cash. In scenario A we will pay cash for one property, and in scenario B we will use the cash as a down payment to purchase the properties with debt in the form of a mortgage. We will presume a 6.5% interest rate amortized over 30 years and a historic appreciation rate of 5.4% per year. For cash flow, we will presume our rent starts at $1,500 per month and the rent appreciates at 3.4% per year. All numbers will be annualized.

Scenario A unleveraged: Purchase a property in cash for $200,000. We then hold that property for 10 years while the property's market value (MV) appreciates over time. Historically, this is about 5.4% per year. After 10 years the market value of the property has appreciated from $200,000 to $338,404, thus appreciating by $138,404 over 10 years.

10 Year MV Projection of One $200,000 Home Paid in Full

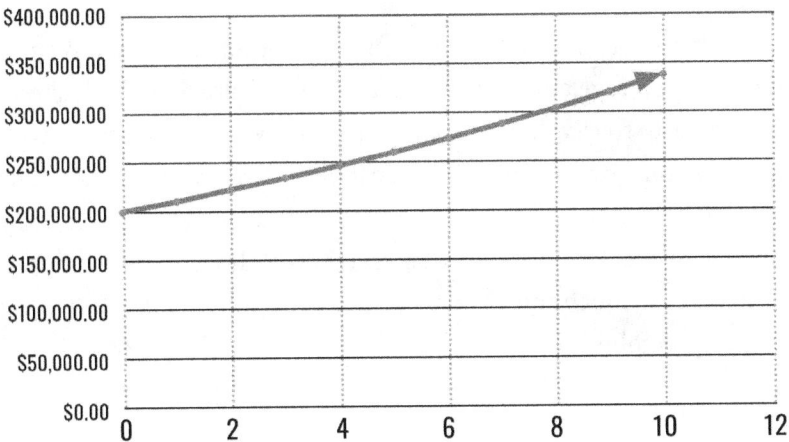

Scenario B leveraged: Here we can buy three properties valued at $200,000 each. To do this we will use three mortgages, each with a 30%

down payment of $60,000. The total out-of-pocket costs for the down payments is $180,000, which leaves $20,000 in cash for reserves. Using our same model, the portfolio value increases $415,213 over the 10-year period. The use of leverage allows the portfolio to work three times as hard for the investor while spending $20,000 less than the unleveraged portfolio.

10 Year MV Projection of 3 $200,000 Homes with Down Payment of $180,000 ($60k Each)

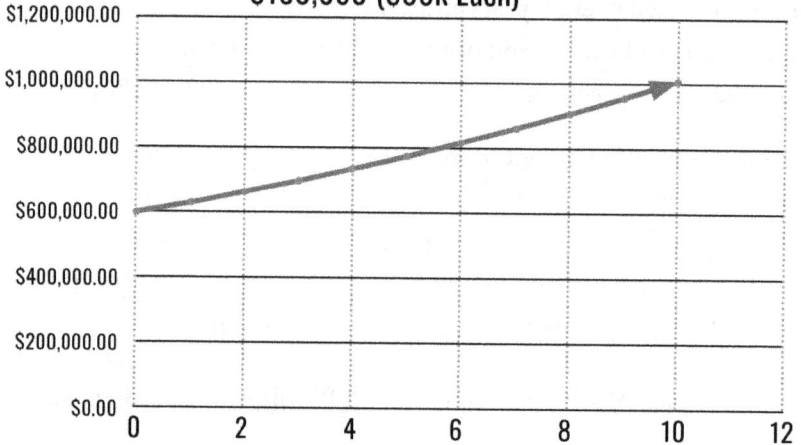

When we factor in the rent cash flows, we add another level of earnings that leverage allows us to multiply. The following graph shows the difference in free cash flow to the portfolio. We have reduced the annual rental income by the annual debt cost of the loans when considering the cash flow differences between the unleveraged and leveraged portfolios. Even with the debt costs, the leveraged portfolio grew much faster and provided for much more revenue over time compared with the unleveraged portfolio.

Annual Portfolio Cash Flow Projections at $1,500 Starting Rent per Property

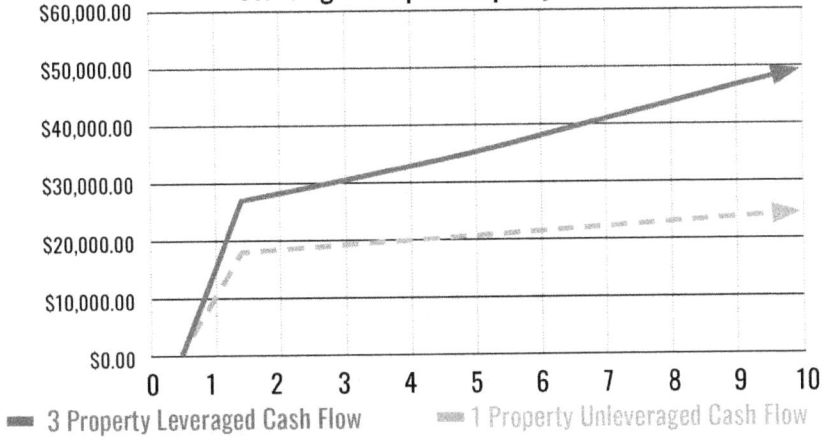

— 3 Property Leveraged Cash Flow   ▪▪▪ 1 Property Unleveraged Cash Flow

In both market value appreciation and in cash flow, the leveraged property significantly outperformed the unleveraged one. The question to ask is by how much. The leveraged portfolio's gross cash flow has generated $375,953 in revenue over 10 years and a market appreciation of $415,213 for a total earnings of $791,166. By contrast, the unleveraged portfolio appreciated by $138,404 and generated a total gross cash flow of $210,191 over the same period for a total of $348,595.

Portfolio Earning Over 10 Years

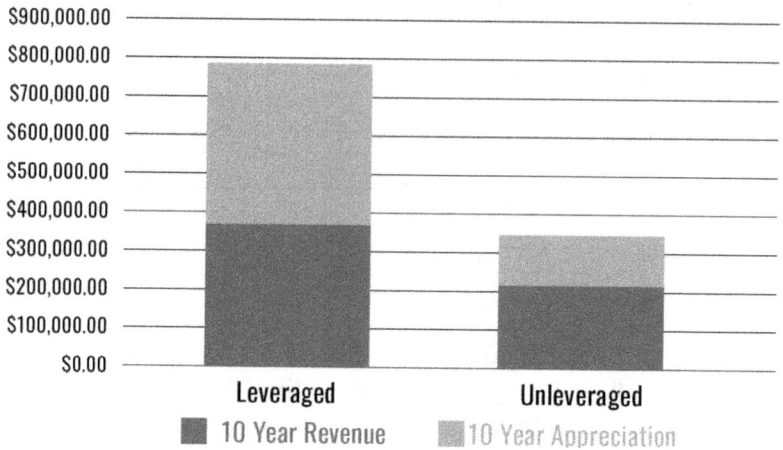

In this example the leveraged portfolio outperformed the unleveraged portfolio by 227% over 10 years.

The Bleak Outlook

Leveraging money is always a balancing act, and experts should be consulted before you borrow money. Borrowers before the real estate crash also sought to leverage money, but were actually under-qualified for loans due to lax underwriting standards, and failed to make mortgage payments.

The outlook in real estate as well as regular life was bleak during these years when we bought our first home only to see the value plummet. News reports blasted gloomy headlines, unemployment rose to an uncomfortable high, and fear overtook the pleasant chatter between neighbors.

An article published by the Oxford Economic Papers titled "The Financial Crisis and the Well-Being of Americans" noted: "The summer of 2008 saw a rise in the unemployment rate from 4.8% in April 2008 to 10.6% at its peak in January 2010, a 4.4% drop in employee compensation over five months in 2009–2010, large stimulus-associated tax credits and rebates, a 4.7% drop of personal disposable income in May 2008 and 1.7% in May 2009, as well as a collapse and subsequent recovery of the stock market—the S&P 500 Index on March 6, 2009, had fallen to 40% of its all-time high of October 2007, and then more than doubled again by the end of 2010. Through the fall in the market and the fall in the prices of housing and of other assets, 60% of households saw their wealth decline between 2007 and 2009, and 25% lost more than half of their wealth."

Sellers could not afford to sell their homes. The amount a seller would gain off the sale of their home simply was not enough with the drastic decrease in home values. They were frozen in place by economic constraints.

Buyers could also not afford to pay what the sellers were asking. The weight of sub-prime mortgages that were not being repaid to the lenders, and the massive losses on Wall Street were just too much for the American consumer to bear.

Chris vividly remembers the 2008 financial market crash, which in reality wasn't one day in particular. The events transpired during his senior-level finance courses, so there was real-time studying of the daily events on Wall Street. Companies were filing for bankruptcy left and right. Freddie Mac and Fannie Mae were taken over by the federal government. (Freddie Mac and Fannie Mae are federally backed home mortgage companies that were created by the US Congress. These companies buy and guarantee mortgages on the secondary market. This allows lenders to offload the mortgages to the federal government in order to keep lending to others.)

Bear Stearns, an investment bank that seemed too big to fail, failed.

Everything in the financial world seemed to be in chaos.

Of course, it isn't as if nobody bought or sold real estate during this time soon after 2008. People get married, divorced, make career changes, grow families, have adult children who move out, and encounter other situations that require they move.

Cash investors also saw lucrative deals arise and bought them. Straight cash home sales were not dependent on the mortgage lending industry, freshly left in ruin. There was, and still is, no credit requirement or income requirement for these buyers. Simply put, if you had the cash, you could buy a property. In fact, cash buyers were able to buy many homes for a deep discount.

Both these situations, with added help from the government in the form of the Troubled Assets Relief Program (TARP), kept the heart of the real estate market beating, albeit faintly and slowly at first. America had to recover from the deep damage that had been done.

Chris graduated from the Terry College of Business with his BBA in finance in 2009 as Céline completed her first year in vet school. He had his eyes set on a career in financial advising without any intent to join the fledgling real estate brokerage that Céline's parents had started in 2007.

He eventually found an entry position as a financial advisor with Waddell & Reed. He obtained his FINRA® Series 7 that allowed him to sell all general securities. He also obtained his FINRA® Series 66 that taught him about the laws for acting as a broker-dealer and investment advisor.

And there we were. Homeowners in our early 20s—a second-year veterinary student and a recent business school graduate starting a commission-based career without immediate income—living on a shoestring budget during the Great Recession. Did we know what we were doing when it came to running a household? No, but we were starting to learn.

CHAPTER 3

LEARNING TO BE A HOMEOWNER

W e started with mantras that were ingrained into our personal philoso-
phies, which were to stay out of unnecessary debt and to live within our
means. We also wanted to protect our credit scores, carefully. Subsequent
real estate purchases depended on our being responsible young adults.

Good vs. Bad Debt

There is bad debt and there is good debt. Knowing the difference can
be extremely difficult when you are peppered with information from
famous financial gurus on TV and radio who constantly preach that all
debt is bad debt.

The easiest and most general way to tell the difference between good
and bad debt is whether the money borrowed is used to purchase an
asset or a liability.

An asset is something that usually increases in worth over time. For
example, a house is an asset in the US. The debt taken out to purchase a
house is usually considered good debt.

On the other hand, a liability is something that decreases in worth
over time (the value lost over time is called depreciation). A car, for

example, is a depreciating asset, even if you prudently buy a solid used car. Other examples are furniture, electronics, and clothing. The debt taken out to purchase a car is considered bad debt despite their utility.

> Note: Paying interest on borrowed money in order to own a liability will take away from money you can invest. You will also have less available cash flow every month. Think carefully before you buy that customized living room set or theater-sized television if you don't have the money to pay in full.

We formed a strong belief that when people incur bad debt, they essentially are robbing their futures for their today. Incremental costs can add up over a lifetime.

We were not perfect young adults, though. Chris had used his credit card for a few months after he graduated in order to maintain a higher standard of living than we could afford. He would use plastic for restaurant meals and other everyday items we did not need. The standard he chose was unsustainable for our income (which was very little as a college student). He quickly realized the challenges involved in maintaining a credit card balance that he could not easily pay back.

We decided that credit cards were not for us because Chris did not have enough self-discipline to maintain the card and pay the balance in full each month. We learned that it's okay to say that credit cards are not for you.

We paid off the entire credit card balance, hid the cards in an inconvenient location, and have remained credit card–free. We have since had to use a credit card to run the day-to-day expenses of owning a real estate brokerage, but the charges are only for business purposes, and the balance is always paid in full monthly. We are more disciplined with accounting now and are not incurring costs on interest.

Inflation was also rampant coming out of the Great Recession years. Everything from utilities needed to keep the house running, to basic necessities such as food, were costing Americans more than they had ever had to pay in their recent memories. We were not immune to the costs either.

Céline created a budget with quarterly reviews from Chris. We carefully adjusted every category and included discretionary spending in the calculations. That said, our discretionary spending was at times a mere $15 per month for both of us. It was tough.

Chris in front of the fireplace where we burned wood for warmth during those early years.

Our budgeting may have been slightly obsessive, but it was so important to not fall into debt other than Céline's federal student loan debt from veterinary school. We held onto this philosophy so tightly that we even bought a cord of wood two years in a row. The wood provided the only heat for us in the winter without the use of our electric furnace, which saved us money. Céline had to study for difficult medical exams while bundled in multiple layers of clothing with a small portable space heater at her feet to keep them from becoming numb. She didn't mind because it was a sacrifice that would make our lives easier in the future.

A trip to the grocery store was also difficult, but doable. Each week, we would allocate $50 toward food for both of us. Meals were written down in a planner, and the ingredients were economical, but healthy. We often made do with basic salads, cheaper cuts of meat such as chicken thighs, and sandwiches for the most part. These meals were quick to make with the limited time Céline had while studying.

We also became DIY experts in home projects.
When we had a house mouse problem, YouTube research on removing them effectively taught Chris how to place traps. This saved us hundreds in exterminator costs during a lean winter. It also taught us how to remove and install kitchen and bath faucets when our old ones became defective.

A small purchase of $200 in tools saved a lot of money compared to hiring a professional. In the first house, we had one basic off-brand home-owner kit with hand tools like screwdrivers, a hammer, tape measure, sockets, wrenches, and pliers. We had a second kit that was an off-brand of power tools. It contained a saw, drill, and flashlight, with a couple of batteries. The quality was awful, but they handled most small tasks like assembling furniture and minor repairs.

One of the added joys of owning a home is the freedom to decorate and use the property the way we wanted to. Yet, with a limited budget, we had to make our dollars stretch here too. Facebook Marketplace had not been developed, so Craigslist was the preferred way to buy secondhand goods online. We would scour the "free" posts and jump on any opportunity we could find. We were able to acquire some decent furniture, barware, exercise equipment, and even a Christmas tree for little to no cost.

One day, our stovetop stopped working. The home warranty we got with the purchase of the townhouse saved us from a large cost to fix it. We paid a total of $50 for a service call, and an electrician spent an hour diagnosing. He repaired a short in the system to have it working again quickly. This kind of repair was something we anticipated and negotiated into the purchase of the property in order to protect ourselves from unexpected, large out-of-pocket expenses.

Instead of turning to a credit card, Chris found odd jobs here and there, even if it meant a small paycheck. One of these jobs was to drive cars onto a platform to be auctioned off at a local car auction. Chris was paid $25 each night he drove, which was only offered two times per month. Still, this was enough to pay a utility bill such as water and keep us out of unnecessary debt. Another job he eventually found was as a manager of an independent cell phone store. This job definitely did not make use of his finance degree and paid a pitiful hourly wage.

Yet, we took every opportunity we had to stay afloat no matter how different the job was from what we had studied at UGA. Our pride was not going to get in the way of making the right decisions for our future. We were willing to get our hands dirty and dig in the mud to do what needed to be done.

The skills we learned to make it through this arduous period in our lives shaped us in wonderful ways. Nevertheless, it was so easy to be tempted to order food from a store down the street when daily schedules seemed too hectic to consider cooking. Indulging in a haircut at a salon was too costly when it could be done at home for free with a pair of scissors. Movie dates were out of the question when we could rent five DVDs for five dollars at the local video rental store, Vision Video. Valentine's Day presents were handmade paper posters with reasons why we loved each other with a home-cooked and thoughtful meal.

We were dedicated to our plan for the future, and we considered the challenges we faced as sacrifices for our family to come.

Chris left his role as a financial advisor due to the economy and was actively looking for different work within the finance sector. The Great Recession told him that the financial advising career was not for him. Those with money to invest were looking for experienced financial advisors. Other people Chris encountered lacked the need for an advisor altogether.

The odd jobs made it easy to look and interview for an opening, which, after two years in the thick of the Great Recession, did not materialize after all. There was a prolonged, eerie quiet in the air with not a single "now hiring" sign in sight.

We are real humans, and we are not perfect by any means. Our pride did affect us in some ways. Céline's father had been watching Chris struggle with his job search throughout this time. Although he offered to pay for Chris's real estate license, Chris declined because of his belief that the right finance job would come.

Our monetary situation then reached even more difficult challenges as time dragged on, as did our stubbornness to stay debt-free. We needed immediate income from Chris in order to continue investing for our future together. We knew we couldn't be wasting our precious time. We were living off Céline's federal student loan while waiting patiently for job market conditions to improve for Chris.

Finally and begrudgingly, Chris obtained his real estate sales license. He joined the family brokerage in September 2010. To this day, he jokingly says that he was pulled into the family brokerage "kicking and screaming."

CHAPTER 4

THE RISE OF SHORT SALES

The Great Recession took its toll on nearly everyone we knew in some way. One day, there was a knock on our front door while Chris was prospecting for real estate leads at home. These leads were few and far between because many in the US could not afford to sell their homes. Much less buy one.

He answered the door without any idea of who it could be. It turned out to be our neighbor who was standing at the doorstep with tears in her eyes. An alarmed Chris listened to her story of how no real estate agent would help her sell her home because she also owed the lender more than her house was worth. She was "underwater" in her mortgage. Every real estate agent she had reached out to would not return her call. She needed a short sale, which is a type of real estate sale frequently used in these underwater situations.

Short sale: A short sale is a sale of a property at an asking price less than the amount owed to the lender on the current owner's mortgage. The lender must agree to accept less than the full payoff amount for a short sale to be approved. Usually, the seller is not allowed to receive any proceeds from the sale unless permitted by the lender.

The lender can either forgive the owner completely or potentially require them to make payments beyond the completion of the short sale. Legislation passed during the Great Recession limited the penalties for homeowners, but many of those protections expired in 2020. Anyone considering a short sale should consult an attorney to understand the possible tax and legal ramifications.

At the time few agents knew how to do a short sale. Yet so many desperate homeowners needed them. The market had been red hot before the 2008 real estate bubble burst. Many new agents had entered the industry in the preceding years to capitalize on the pre-crash momentum. Easy mortgages meant lots of sales and little need to learn how to do a short sale before this time; consequently, most agents did not have this skill.

In a traditional real estate sale, the property is sold for a value greater than the debt currently owed on the property. Often, this means that the seller will receive enough money from the sale to pay off the balance of their mortgage loan and walk away with a check for the remaining balance—or equity.

When the property is being sold as a short sale, the seller must first make a case to, and get the approval of, their mortgage lender. The seller must show that they can no longer afford to pay the monthly amount. The lender must then approve a contract in which the seller may be able to sell the property "short" of the amount the seller owes.

The approval process requires weeks or months of communication and document submission. Back-and-forth talks with the lender must happen for the seller's case to be fully evaluated. The lender will look at the seller's stated hardships and financial position along with the property's valuation to determine short sale approval. Sellers avoid foreclosure and get out of a difficult financial commitment in return.

Compared to a short sale, foreclosure is typically reported in greater severity on credit reports and precludes the individual from obtaining a new mortgage loan for a much longer timeline. Credit damage from a short sale can sometimes be overcome in as little as two years instead of five, depending on the location and lender.

Understanding the basics, Chris contacted our neighbor's lender and received their instructions for processing a short sale. He was to list the property, place it under contract, and upload the documents into a program called Equator—a multi-bank short sale processing platform. Equator was also his system for communicating with the lenders.

Over the next few months, he processed the short sale with a buyer from California. The sale was a headache and there was much back-and-forth with the lender to complete the deal. It took an astounding 97 days to process from contract to closing.

We look back at this first short sale as a blessing to both our next-door neighbor and our family. As we stated before, real estate transactions were scarce after the real estate crash. The commission from this short sale was enough to tide us over to the next sale Chris was able to produce. He was able to market himself as knowledgeable on short sales, and he helped many more families get out of bad mortgage situations because few agents were qualified to help them. There was a sense of genuine relief for the sellers when they were able to escape what seemed an inevitable foreclosure.

Our neighbor kept in touch with us after the economy recovered. She was doing well when we caught up over the phone and was living in close proximity to the townhouse she sold as a short sale in Athens. Her credit was damaged, but not beyond repair. She was able to qualify for a rental immediately and moved to a location about five minutes away. The move also let her child remain in the same school district. She was able to get a new job and restructure her finances without the underwater mortgage payment looming over her head.

Brittany Denmark Purcell (from left), Nakia Brooks, Ursula Johnson Lowther, and Chris Evans, panelists in the Short Sale Mastermind Session, October 21, 2011.

Chris, now armed with the know-how for processing these short sales, was ready to seize an opportunity to help others in need.

SEO (search engine optimization) was relatively easy in 2011. With a Blogger account, anyone could achieve being displayed on the first page of Google back then. All you had to do was have photos and 600+ words about a concise topic. Chris spent countless hours into early mornings building a short sale website, and he became the area's short sale expert. In addition, Chris pursued additional certifications in short sales and coordinated special training events in these types of sales for Sellect Realty agents.

Chris shared the content he was writing about short sales with the Athens community. He was soon invited to contribute his knowledge to a forum and then for a local NBC affiliate website.

These engagements within the local community presented Chris with multiple opportunities to sell homes. He quickly built his business to over $25M in sales volume in four years. Economic recovery was finally starting to pick up, and America was on its way to digging itself out from the Great Recession. And so were we.

In October 2011, he was invited to his first professional speaking event—something he had always wanted to do. Chris was to be a panelist along with two other agents. The topic was, of course, processing short sales. The other panelists and Chris collectively felt the need to educate peers on this topic as a service to the industry. The housing market desperately needed to be rebuilt from the damage of the housing crash of 2008.

The room was packed to the brim. Every seat was taken with people lining the back wall and into the hallway. The event was only scheduled for an hour, but ran for two because there were so many questions from the audience.

Chris and the other panelists discussed everything possible, inside and out. They covered the short sale hardship requirements, common processing quirks, and response times unique to each lender. The agents then shared tales from the trenches to educate others on what short sale scenarios were approved and ones that weren't.

The housing market would eventually recover to home values that had not been seen since 2009, but only by 2014.

The real-world ability to make an impact on someone's future through real estate set Chris on fire. He knew from the short sale speaking panel that there were many more buyers and sellers he needed to help. They needed education on the best options for them and their individual situations.

The commissions Chris earned helping others jumped significantly from 2011 to 2012. He felt as if he had found a footing as we were entering the next phase of life. We finally had a little breathing room. This was just in time, too, because we planned to be married.

CHAPTER 5

BECOMING A LANDLORD

In the summer of 2012, Céline graduated from the University of Georgia College of Veterinary Medicine. She immediately took a position as an associate veterinarian in a small Appalachian Trail town in North Carolina two weeks after graduation. We were married one month after she received her diploma.

This move to North Carolina put our grit to the test, again. Chris was midway through his second year in real estate and finally able to get some traction in sales. The move out of state would require him to commute during the week to metro Atlanta to be near his clients, and back to North Carolina to be with Céline on the weekends. Céline stayed in North Carolina almost exclusively to be near her practice. Chris lived with Céline's parents in Georgia during the weekdays.

In addition to this new, long-distance marriage, we had to learn how to be landlords for the first time for the townhouse in Athens. We weren't ready to commit to buying a property in North Carolina when Céline had just started a new career. We did not know if the practice was a fit that would keep us there for years to come.

Chris was able to find a small rental home in the Nantahala National Forest to call home base. We decided to rent it for at least a year to test out the North Carolina waters and job.

Chris's real estate licensing gave him a general sense of what needed to be done to become a landlord to rent out the townhouse we owned in Athens. Our property was far enough away from campus to discourage a majority of undergraduate students, but close enough to campus to attract graduate students or teaching assistants. We would come to learn that these tenants often sign multi-year commitments, which reduce the cost of turnover, in our experience.

He put the Athens townhome up for rent and received a qualified tenant within a few weeks. We do not address tenant selection in detail for confidentiality to protect our past tenants, but there are many things to consider when choosing a tenant that minimizes the risk of default on a rental payment. Some of these considerations include career type, income, rental history, credit scores, and background checks.

A landlord must also abide by all local, county, and state regulations for their rental property. Landlords may be subject to federal laws including credit, privacy, and business laws as well as US Fair Housing regulations. For this reason we recommend that a licensed, professional property manager be used for rental properties.

Fair Housing: Federal Fair Housing prohibits discrimination under protected classes such as marital status, gender, and more. Occupation is not a protected class. You can discriminate against careers that will do a disservice to you. For instance, we would personally never rent to an attorney. Why? We didn't want the added headache of dealing with their sometimes too-thorough criticism and potentially making changes on the standard Georgia Association of REALTORS leasing contracts.

Attorneys have made some of the most difficult tenants we have ever dealt with. The pain of dealing with an overly aggressive attorney who demanded changes on the lease was not worth our time. Sorry. We don't mean any offense, but being a landlord is a business. These were not tenants we wanted to deal with.

Our current real estate portfolio inventory (2012)

Fee simple townhouse now rented to a tenant four years after purchasing our first home.

Hiring a property manager would have cost us around 10% of the gross rent per month. We decided to manage our property ourselves since Chris was a licensed real estate agent. Even though we only had one property in the portfolio so far, and we owned the property to be managed, we wanted our tenants to have a professional experience.

We implemented software (the most affordable and within budget we could find) to help us in the accounting and financial record keeping of the townhouse. Sellect Realty, our real estate brokerage, still uses an updated version of this software today.

This software gave us the ability to collect tenant rent from their checking accounts every month, which saved us time. Our management software also gave us the ability to give each tenant a unique portal. They could even submit maintenance requests through the portal. The software has kept a record of these requests to this day, tracks payments made in order to issue 1099 tax documents to vendors, and processes the direct deposit of money to our owners' accounts each month.

The number of checking accounts (trust or escrow accounts) required of a landlord depends on state regulatory structure and the organizational structure of your company. For example, checking accounts and trust account management is regulated heavily for real estate brokers compared to an unlicensed property management company (yes, they exist).

We are required to keep three trust accounts at Sellect Realty, our licensed real estate brokerage in Georgia. The first account is a security deposit account. This account keeps the tenants' deposits separate from all other operations. A second account is a rental trust account. The account collects the rents from multiple tenants. The last account is the operating account. This account contains money intended for business operations.

Why is it so important to have so many accounts? When monthly rent is received, there are many parties that have "claim" to the rent funds:

- The property manager (if not self-managed) has claim to their fee for management services.
- A contractor may have a claim. For example, a plumber may have claim to a repair invoice.
- The owner has claim to the remainder of the funds in the account each month.

Placing funds into designated trust accounts properly discloses that you do not "claim" all the funds in that account for yourself as an individual. Designated trust accounts will protect an individual's claim to funds within the account if the business experiences loss.

More important information we learned as first-time landlords is the 75% rule: When you rent a property to someone with a long-term lease, banks can count 75% of the gross (total) rent you receive each month as "additional income." This is important to keep in mind when qualifying for a subsequent purchase to add to your real estate portfolio.

This means that you don't have to be financially capable of paying for every property in your portfolio each month by yourself. Rather, the rental income can count as additional income when obtaining the loan.

We learned quite a bit with our first rental. The knowledge gained would come in handy as we grew our portfolio.

See the website (*www.hshbrands.com/FromTheGroundUp*) for rental marketing tips, a new tenant checklist, property management tips, and more.

CHAPTER 6

RENTER TO OWNER, AGAIN

The job in North Carolina didn't work out for Céline. It turned out to be largely a retirement town with septuagenarian and octogenarian residents. The pet owners saw her as a fresh veterinarian who was too young to be a doctor at 26 and did not seem to believe her knowledge in medicine. Further, she and her employer were not on the same page.

Céline decided that it was time to leave North Carolina, so she moved back to Georgia to be with Chris. This was probably also a blessing in disguise because the three-hour commutes for him to North Carolina on the weekends were taking a heavy toll.

However, we could not purchase another house right away when Céline returned to Georgia. We had to have a long history of being a landlord at the time to qualify for our next mortgage. This is no longer a requirement to buy a second property, but we needed to show proof at the time. Regulations have changed since then.

Céline's parents were gracious and understanding enough to welcome us back into their home until we were able to obtain the needed history as a landlord. We are forever grateful that they took us in (although it was slightly embarrassing) and intended to only stay the shortest time possible.

We understand that not everyone has opportunities such as the one we had, and did not waste a single day. We saved everything we could with fervor to purchase our next property and take the burden off her parents.

A crash course in tax planning was also necessary because we were both now defined as self-employed for tax purposes. This is also known as a 1099 employee. Applying for a mortgage loan as a married couple who are both self-employed is different from applying for one when you are both W-2 employees.

Risk management is always a concern for mortgage companies when considering loan applicants. Borrowers with consistent, recurring income are safer for lending companies (this is called a W-2 employee). Sufficient credit scores and monthly income are required in addition to ensure that the monthly mortgage payment will be paid in a timely manner.

We weren't W-2 employees. As such, we needed two years' worth of tax records with enough income from both of us to assure the lending company that the monthly mortgage payments would be paid. We took careful planning and the time to show that we were not a risk to the lending company.

W-2 vs. 1099

There is a stark difference in finances and requirements for lending depending on the way an individual earns their income. Let's look at the two most common ways here.

W-2: A W-2 is an IRS form that is completed by hourly or salaried employees of a company. There is an employer-employee relationship where the employer has control of the employee's tasks and behavior when they are at work. The employer can dictate attire, hours, and anything else the law permits in this type of relationship. The employer is buying obedience and results from the employee. In return, the employer pays taxes, FICO, workers' comp (when applicable), and possibly other benefits.

A mortgage company may accept 30 or 60 days of paystubs for a W-2 employee, but will require two full years of tax returns for self-employed individuals. The two years are averaged to give a more accurate reflection of the business earnings.

1099: A 1099 is an IRS form that is used for independent contractor relationships. When an independent contractor relationship is formed, the person working is not considered an employee. Technically, they are their own business that another business is contracting with to complete a job. The hiring entity does not pay taxes, benefits, workers' comp insurance, or anything else on behalf of the contractor. The hiring entity, in turn, is unable to dictate when or in what style the job gets done, but can require that the work be done to a certain level of standards. The hiring entity in an independent contractor relationship also cannot dictate to the contractor to come to the office to work, but they can require a certain level of training.

The 1099 contractor can have a mix of salary, commissions, or owner distributions depending on their structure. The income may be higher in certain times of the year than others. (An example would be tax accountants who are busy during tax season.) Uneven income distributions may make it hard for lenders to determine how risky the borrower is, so they average the income over a longer period of time.

Therefore, as a self-employed, 1099 family, we had to do some serious planning with our taxes to make sure we were able to qualify for our next house. Our income needed to be high enough, averaged across two years of tax returns, to show that we had an acceptable adjusted gross income to qualify for a mortgage.

Lenders also needed to consider our debt-to-income ratio in order for us to qualify for another mortgage loan.

Debt-to-income ratio (DTI): The percentage of gross monthly income that goes toward paying off debt each month. Lenders use DTI as a tool to determine how much borrowing capacity an individual has when taking out a loan. Generally, an individual with a low debt-to-income ratio is considered a financially responsible individual. They are more likely to manage their monthly debt payments effectively since they have more available cash flow to apply toward their living expenses.

For an average person, a low DTI usually means they have sustainable credit card debt, auto loans, or mortgages.

We did not have credit card debt from the lessons we had learned earlier in life, and always paid cash for automobiles to own them outright. Our DTI was acceptable because of our strict spending habits and determination to not take on any bad debts that could be avoided.

While we sorted out the necessary paperwork, we started the search for the second home to purchase. Here is a list of what we looked for in the property itself.

Our Must-Have List for Our Second Property

- Fee simple.
- Well maintained.
- Reasonable HOA costs (if there is an HOA).
- Ability to rent the property to a tenant in the future.
- Reasonable property taxes.
- Two sinks in the master bathroom.

Céline was pregnant with our first child in the middle of the search. Sometimes life doesn't wait for the best time, nor is there a best time to begin with. She decided to give birth to our child before continuing with her career in veterinary medicine because the field was slow to recover from the Great Recession. She would also be astoundingly gravid while interviewing for positions as an associate veterinarian, although that shouldn't have affected the hiring process. Yet, we all know it silently can.

She started helping out with Sellect Realty while waiting for the new arrival.

On July 18, 2013, our first child, James, was born healthy and ready to take on the world. We enjoyed every minute as new parents, but most importantly, Céline was just relieved for the rough pregnancy to be over.

We found a property within our budget that fit our needs. The house was located in the northern suburbs of Georgia in a city called Acworth. It was almost six years after our first home purchase in Athens. The second house was somewhat close to Céline's parents, but not as close as we would have liked it to be. The house had charming curb appeal and everything on our list. Except that one darned sink in the master bathroom. Oh well. We agreed it was a close enough match and that you can't win every time you find a suitable property.

Our second home purchase in Acworth.

The purchase of the second property was a game changer for us in planning for our retirement. We could now claim a homestead exemption on our primary residence while claiming depreciation on our investment property.

Our current real estate portfolio inventory (2014)

1. Fee simple townhouse rented to a tenant.
2. Single-family residential home as a primary residence bought six years after purchasing our first home and two years after officially becoming real estate investors with rental properties.

Céline's father had a sudden health emergency in 2014 where he came close to losing his life. He had a 2% chance of survival, and lived. This meant that her father had to immediately retire from the real estate brokerage he founded in 2007—Sellect Realty. Céline's mother retired along with him in order to take care of him during his recovery.

Chris stepped up to the plate and enrolled to obtain his real estate broker license. In the spring of 2015 he passed the licensing exam and assumed his new role as the new principal broker of Sellect Realty. The brokerage had grown from a basement office in Céline's parents' house to a small upper-floor office rental in a nearby office park, then to the bottom floor of a larger office rental of the same office park.

It was time for a new chapter in our lives.

CHAPTER 7

HERMIT CRABBING

Our family grew again in 2016 when our daughter Scarlett was born. Our home in the northern suburbs of Atlanta was starting to feel a little bit more crowded with a total of two children, two adults, and three dogs. Talk about a full house!

We made do until we were bursting out of the house's seams. Between the preschool drop-offs and pickups, traveling to work, and going to visit Céline's parents, we were spending too much of our time traveling in a vehicle. We needed a property that was closer to our daily activities in life.

We decided to buy another property as a primary residence as soon as we had enough money gathered for another down payment. And once again, we set our criteria for our third property.

Our Must-Have List for Our Third Property
- Fee simple.
- Well maintained.
- Reasonable HOA costs (if there is an HOA).
- Ability to rent the property to a tenant in the future.
- Reasonable property taxes.

- High-scoring and supportive school district.
- Closer to our daily life activities.
- Two sinks in the master bathroom.

A school district was now on the list because our son was nearing elementary school age and would be attending public school.

You may also be wondering why this chapter's title is called hermit crabbing. Well, it's a fun term that we came up with to describe how we acquired properties.

The Hermit Crabbing Method

The concept of hermit crabbing is loosely based on the hermit crab. As hermit crabs grow bigger, a new shell is needed to accommodate their growing size. Hermit crabs also do not grow the shells they live in themselves. Instead, they find empty shells that are no longer inhabited by other animals. Their method of changing homes is much akin to homes people live in, and reasons for moving.

However, we are not hermit crabs that find free housing on the ocean floor, and most often we finance our homes with mortgages. We coined this fun term to describe the method in which we acquired three residential properties up to this point. Each time we outgrew the house, we looked for a new shell while renting out the old ones.

Lease It, Don't Sell

Many buyers think that when they need to move, the only way to qualify for a new mortgage is with the sale and proceeds from the current home they live in. However, this is not the case. The lease of their previous home can also qualify under certain conditions.

So why don't more sellers rent out the homes they are moving out of? We think that sellers choose not to lease from fear of the unknown, the thought that they must roll their equity into a subsequent property, or do not want to pay for property management. In addition, the sellers may not know how to manage property as a business, how to interact with potential tenants, and are intimidated by the daunting process of having to evict someone.

Rarely do we encounter someone who has regretted buying a property. Instead, we most often see regret from people selling properties. The most common comment we hear is, "I wish I never sold that property. If I had it today, it would be worth $_____."

Financing the third home purchase required us to lease out our current house before the next property's mortgage loan would be approved.

Our loan officer was instrumental during the process of acquiring our third property. He educated us on the underwriting standards we would need for our situation. He also told us the exact amount of rent we would need to receive on the property we were moving out of to qualify for financing the third property.

We were told that we were required to secure a tenant, sign a lease, and share a copy of the first month's rent check with our lender. Following the 75% rule that we briefly mentioned in chapter 4, we were able to offset the debt and have additional income to help us qualify.

The 75% Rule (Fannie Mae Rule B3-3.5-02)

The 75% rule is the Fannie Mae underwriting guideline B3-3.5-02. This section of the underwriting guideline for mortgage loans covers how rental income can be used to offset the debt incurred by owning the rental property.

The general takeaway from the guideline is that you can count 75% of the rent amount from a property as additional income when obtaining a mortgage on a new property. That can be a bit confusing, so let's look at an example to demonstrate how this works. For simplicity, we are not factoring in full underwriting criteria, but rather a simplified scenario to demonstrate the relationship between the rental cash flow and general qualifications for a new mortgage for a subsequent property. For accurate advice on how this works, speak with your mortgage professional.

EXAMPLE: Bill and Linda make $75,000 per year combined. They own a home with a mortgage on it and are wanting to purchase another home, which they intend to use as a primary residence. Their current mortgage payment is $1,250 per month.

Bill and Linda are speaking with their mortgage lender about whether they would need to sell their current home, or if it would be possible to rent it out.

If they sell their house, they will pay off the mortgage on their property and receive the remaining balance as income. This process removes debt from their DTI, which allows them to qualify for the new loan. By removing debt, they are free to replace it with another loan for a different property.

On the other hand, what if they would like to consider keeping their current home as an investment? If Bill and Linda have enough in savings for the purchase of the next property, then they do not need to sell their existing house as long as their debt-to-income ratio shows enough room to absorb the new mortgage for the next home.

Using the 75% rule, we know that they would need to rent their existing home for $1,667 to add enough income to their calculations to offset the debt payment of the full $1,250. See the chart showing where income increases from $75,000 to $90,000 annually. The debt remains, but the lender can count the additional rent as income to offset the debt obligation.

What if their existing property rents for $2,000 per month? By calculating 75% of the $2,000 rent as additional income ($1,500), we have not only offset the existing debt payments of $1,250, but they have added an additional $250 per month as income, which can be used to help them qualify for a slightly nicer home on the next property.

Example to Show How Rent Increases Qualifying Income

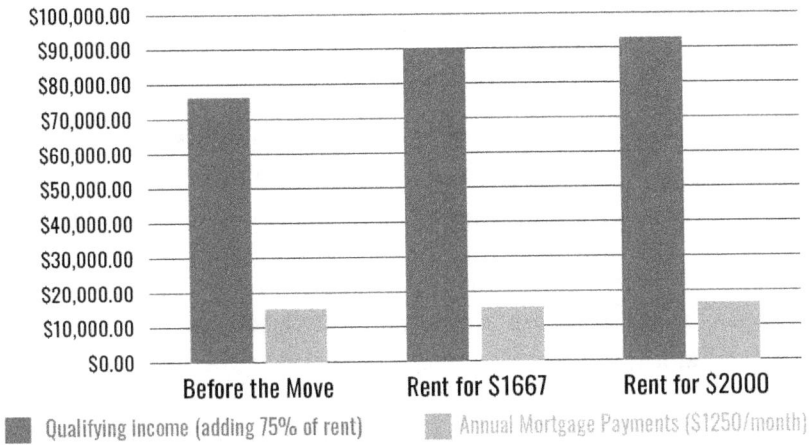

Which scenario would make more sense to you?

We finally started looking for the third property, and shortly thereafter put one under contract. It was closer to where our daily life activities were, had a pool, creek, and wooded yard. It also had, finally, two sinks.

However, the downside was that it was incredibly below the street level. The driveway sloped at an extreme angle downward, and the house sat at least 10 feet below grade. Neither of us liked it too much because we always consider exit strategies when purchasing property. We had to think about how well the house would sell if we needed to offload it from our portfolio. You never know what life will throw at you in the future. We had to be prepared, just in case.

During our due diligence, Céline found a different home that was for sale by owner (FSBO) by complete chance. She had continued to look even after we had a contract on a house because the steep driveway and structure below grade did not sit well with her instincts. Georgia is a caveat emptor, or "buyer beware" state, and we had the right to terminate for any reason within this time period.

We toured the FSBO property Céline found, and she was immediately sold. She turned to Chris and told him without hesitation, "This is the one." It was an almost perfect fit for our needs, had a flat driveway, and was not below grade.

Chris expressed his interest to the seller and negotiated the sales contract face-to-face with her in the kitchen. We left the house with an offer drafted and waited for her to electronically sign overnight.

The next morning we had a signed contract on the second property as we left town for a conference and long weekend with our kids in Orlando, Florida.

We used our time on the road to carefully compare both properties: the one we already had under contract, and the FSBO home we just submitted an offer for. We considered the locations, amenities, and our opinions of the changes that we could expect for the surrounding areas over the next 20 years. We agreed that the FSBO home would be the most fitting home for our needs and terminated the contract for the house with the steep driveway.

Do you want to know what the FSBO property didn't have? The master bathroom didn't have two sinks. Darn it! The pros still outweighed the cons. We closed in 2017.

Our current real estate portfolio inventory (2017)

1. Fee simple townhouse rented to a tenant.
2. Single-family residential home rented to a tenant.
3. Single-family residential home as a primary residence purchased nine years after purchasing our first home and five years after officially becoming real estate investors with rental properties.

It had been three years since our purchase of the second property. This was half the time it took to go from one to two properties. We settled into the new house, and James started attending the local elementary school. When Scarlett was a little over one year old, we had a surprise pregnancy. Amélie Clare was born in 2018. Life happens.

CHAPTER 8

THE OFFICE

Y ou would think from our past buying habits that we would have looked for a larger house to accommodate the additional child. We did not. We were already settled in the area, James enjoyed the school, and we knew that we would want our children to attend the nearby high school. We were staying put.

What did we do instead? We started to think about our office rental situation. How could we promote homeownership when we were still renting an office ourselves? We felt like hypocrites because we told renters they should buy in order to better themselves. Renting office space had to stop for us—not only for the benefits of ownership, but also to live by what we preach.

Céline's parents agreed that an office purchase was an idea to pursue to reduce the number of liabilities the company had. After all, they were still majority owners of the brokerage they founded, even though Chris was the principal broker.

Here is a list of the criteria we had in looking for an office to buy:

Our Must-Have List for Our Office Purchase
- Well maintained.
- Convenient location.
- Reasonable HOA costs (if there is an HOA).

- Ability to rent the property to a tenant in the future.
- Reasonable property taxes.

Generally, commercial real estate can be a solid investment. The tenants stay in place longer, the maintenance and taxes can be passed through to the tenant, and there are fewer regulations controlling the landlord-tenant relationship.

The largest barrier to entry is the cost. Not only are commercial buildings more expensive, but they have higher mortgage payments and longer vacancy times. A residential mortgage can be spread over 30 years; whereas, a commercial loan is commonly made for 20 or 25 years. This makes the payment much higher.

Commercial buildings also have much higher vacancy times. They can sit vacant for months or years before finding the right tenant. This means the landlord must be able to afford the carrying cost of the property while there are no rents coming in from a tenant. This is why it's common practice for investors to start in residential real estate before migrating to commercial once their finances are able to afford commercial.

When buying residential real estate, we have regulations that put certain disclosure requirements in place for the seller that cover property defects and environmental hazards. There are also common protections for buyers. The protections most often used are the financing contingency, appraisal contingency, and contingency on sale of existing property.

Commercial real estate is different from residential real estate. From an oversight level, there are more protections and regulations designed to protect consumer buyers purchasing residential real estate than there are for businesses buying commercial real estate.

These properties in the commercial category are also subject to the Comprehensive Environmental Response, Compensation, and Liability

Act (CERCLA). This is also known as the "Superfund." According to the EPA's website (https://www.epa.gov/superfund/superfund-regulations), "This law created a tax on the chemical and petroleum industries and provided broad Federal authority to respond directly to releases or threatened releases of hazardous substances that may endanger public health or the environment."

Essentially, the owner of any contaminated property may be required to bear the cost of remediation from any contamination on their property. This is done even if the contamination was caused by a previous owner.

Commercial properties often go through several inspections to determine whether any contamination on the property is likely. An Environmental Site Assessment Phase I (ESA I) is an inspection that reviews the historical use of the property to determine whether there is any likelihood of contamination from hazardous materials or industrial solvents and the like. A property that was used as an office complex would be less likely to contaminate the earth than a chemical company, but an ESA I may look into an office owned or leased by a chemical company to determine whether any chemicals were stored on premises.

When possible contamination is likely, the assessor for the Phase I ESA may require a Phase II ESA. Phase II is much more invasive and costly. Where a Phase I will include a site inspection and historical analysis, Phase II may include dozens to hundreds of core samples from around the property grounds. A small car dealership we represented in 2022 was quoted over $10,000 for a Phase II ESA, so these can be costly.

Commercial appraisals are less of a focal point than they are in the residential side since the value of the property is highly dependent on revenue generation.

The commercial property buyer will sort out their financing well in advance of a contract or during their due diligence period for most commercial transactions. We refinanced our primary residence, one of our rentals, and added a portion of what we had saved up to see if we had enough for a down payment for the commercial loan. It was still not enough. Well, we had to get creative this time because we needed to stop renting office space.

Céline's grandfather had passed away in 2017 at an amazing age of 92 and left his house to his three adult daughters. Her mother bought the other two sisters' portions of the home and extensively renovated the property to turn it into a rental for monthly income.

Céline's grandfather's renovated home near the Atlanta Braves stadium.

The property was located near a developing area with increasing tourism. The Atlanta Braves had recently built a new baseball stadium within walking distance of the house. Although the property was older, it had just been renovated, and also had sentimental memories for Céline.

This is how we got creative in making up the remainder of the down payment necessary to buy an office building. We bought Céline's grandfather's house from her parents for a fair market value. Her parents then used the proceeds they gained from the sale of this house to pay off other liabilities they had. Additionally, a portion of the proceeds from the sale was gifted to us to bridge the gap in the amount necessary for the down payment to buy the commercial building.

It was a win-win situation for everyone involved.

Eleven years after purchasing our first home and eight years after officially becoming real estate investors with rental properties, our portfolio exceeded a milestone: $1 million in market valuation.

In the same year, Céline obtained her real estate license to join Chris in running the brokerage. She was no longer just helping out.

Our current real estate portfolio inventory (2019)
1. Fee simple townhouse rented to a tenant.
2. Single-family residential home rented to a tenant.
3. Single-family residential home as a primary residence.
4. Single-family residential home rented to a tenant 11 years after purchasing our first home and seven years after officially becoming real estate investors with rental properties.

Céline found an office complex in 2019 that was perfect for the real estate brokerage. It was far larger than anything we had ever purchased and sufficient to run a successful business. It had enough rooms to have a classroom, conference room, personal offices, administrative office, kitchen, workroom, storage, and a full media studio for our agents to create original content and promote their real estate business. The company had also grown to include commercial real estate services, so the building could accommodate a commercial team as well.

We were finally out of renting anything—housing to live in and an office to work out of. Monthly payments were no longer going to pay off another individual or company's mortgage. We would realize the equity. In addition, we would be able to sell the property for a profit (if we maintained it well, and the value increased over time) if we ever needed to.

Our current real estate portfolio inventory (2019)
1. Townhouse rented to a tenant.
2. Single-family residential home rented to a tenant.
3. Single-family residential home as a primary residence.
4. Single-family residential home rented to a tenant.
5. Commercial office for our real estate brokerage purchased 11 years after purchasing our first home and seven years after officially becoming real estate investors with rental properties.

CHAPTER 9

THE BUSINESS OWNER IN A PANDEMIC

The new office move was ready to be tackled with the closing behind us. We had previously researched what was needed of us to own and utilize a commercial building and found that the needs are quite different when compared to a residential move.

Commercial office moves are much more involved than the residential moves. Here are just a few of the tasks we had to consider:

- Set up basic utilities such as electricity and water.
- Obtain/update records with secretary of state.
- Update address records.
- Notify past clients, customers, and vendors.
- Update all online media as well as postings.
- Build out the rooms for use.
  - Install and program commercial phone system.
  - Set up network for high-speed internet.
  - Install multiple printers, scanners, and computers.
  - Assemble and install any new furniture.
  - Decorate.

- Handle permitting (building occupancy/requirements).
  - Initial fire marshal inspection.
  - Implement all safety requirements.
  - Pass a second fire marshal inspection.
  - Obtain a Certificate of Occupancy.

The office building we purchased for the new home of Sellect Realty.

Here are more specifics of moving into commercial real estate space:

Basic utilities: Much like a residential property, commercial office buildings also have utilities. The same power, gas, and water companies that serve the surrounding communities are used. Utilities may be managed and paid by the tenant, owner, the property management company, or through an association (similar to a residential condominium association).

The utilities will often require a guarantor in case of nonpayment, and that's usually the property owner with a high credit score. If the utility accounts are placed solely in the business name without a personal guarantor, then the business itself will likely require a credit score or face thousands of dollars' worth of deposits to establish service.

Business credit scores: These credit scores are secured by applying with companies like Dun & Bradstreet. Firms such as D&B will audit the financial records of the business and rate the business based on its financial performance (https://www.dnb.com/resources/business-credit-report.html).

Internet: Covering 4,500 square feet of office space with a strong Wi-Fi signal and speed was essential for productivity. We opted for a mesh network, which worked exceptionally well. A mesh network is one that has a series of Wi-Fi repeaters that operate on the same network ID. It was a lower-cost option compared with installing multiple access points throughout the building.

Business registration: The secretary of state oversees the registration of domestic and foreign businesses for each state. A business is considered foreign when headquartered in another state. A domestic business is headquartered within the state of registration. Each state has unique procedures, and business requirements may vary. Owners should consult an attorney to determine what is specifically required in their locale.

Business license: Also known as an occupation tax certificate. This document is issued by various levels of government at the local, state, and federal levels based on the type of business itself. The license certifies a business as safe to operate. Some municipalities may require a business license for each rental property.

Update address records: We never realized how many links, publications, and directories our business was already published in until we started to update our business address and contact information. It is a time-consuming process to update the information, but it must be done, often individually and by hand. Make sure this is completed in a timely manner so that important mail is not sent to past addresses. Mail forwarding with the United States Postal Service helps, but this service ends after one year of use.

Telecommunications: A communication system was needed for such a large office space. It was nearly impossible to travel from one end of the building to the other in time to transfer a phone call by foot. We also needed to be able to page individual offices with the press of a button.

We chose to use the MiTel system because the previous owner left it for us as part of our commercial purchase. This telephone system also lets us use an auto-attendant. An auto-attendant is an answering service that will pick up an incoming call and direct the caller to one of our various departments within the brokerage.

Many businesses may not need a fancy system, and cell phones may suffice. Google Voice phone numbers can easily be forwarded to personal cell phones and is free to use.

Permitting: We required site visits from the fire marshal to ensure building compliance before we could officially occupy the building. This permitting step with the fire marshal was difficult and time-consuming.

We fumbled through the process by visiting three different government office buildings before we got the correct information. It was found that our county (Cobb) has two different government departments that we had to work with before they would issue a Certificate of Occupancy.

Certificate of Occupancy: A document issued by local government that legally allows for the occupation of a residential or commercial building. Commonly issued after construction, change in use of a property (for example, our fee simple townhouse that had been converted from apartments) or change in ownership of commercial property.

Check with your local governing body for specific instructions to ensure that you have the correct requirements for your commercial property. Give yourself plenty of time for this certification process.

Then, news of the COVID-19 pandemic came. We suddenly had an office that nobody wanted to visit because we were all too afraid to be within close proximity of each other.

There was a lot of fear of the unknown when the virus was first announced through the media to the world. Common conversations between colleagues questioned what everyday life might look like in the near future. Would mandatory quarantines be the new normal? How does an agent show a house when everyone is scared of getting sick? Did we just buy an office and set it up for it to sit useless?

Fortunately, our building did not need substantial modification to meet our new social distancing needs. The building was large, and there were enough individual rooms.

It was March 2020 when we received notice that our office would need to close. The US government asked that all nonessential workers (businesses that did not provide essential services like health care or staples like groceries) stay at home while they learned more about the new virus. We quickly locked down by directing all agents and staff to start working from home. Chris was the sole individual working from the office building during the shutdown. He worked to answer questions, create and implement strategies, and find ways to pull our brokerage through the crisis.

Two weeks turned to three months. Then, the US government reclassified the real estate industry as an essential service. The new classification allowed real estate agents to work through the COVID lockdown. People needed housing as they could not indefinitely stop their life events. They continued to get married, divorce, have children, move, be relocated, change jobs, retire, and pass away.

A new real estate market forced our brokerage to change our angle in business, mainly because of a 0% federal funds rate by the Federal Open

Market Committee (FOMC). The zero rate was intended to re-engage the economic engine in America after the three-month shutdown. Mortgage rates are closely tied to the federal funds rate. This meant that the interest rates for consumer mortgages such as a 30-year conventional loan were at an all-time low. It cost little to borrow money, and people wanted to capitalize on the opportunity to own.

There was also an ongoing, 10-year history of under-building in the US that followed the 2008 Great Recession. These situations made finding a property to purchase quite difficult. Homeowners, in turn, did not want to sell in fear of not having another home to buy, which exacerbated the supply situation even more. In numbers, our local Multiple Listing Service (MLS) had its inventory reduced to a mere 1.1-month supply. To put that into perspective, a balanced market for our area has between 3 and 4 months' supply.

Multiple Listing Service: A service commonly referred to as the MLS. This is where a real estate agent representing a seller will advertise a property for sale. Agents representing a buyer will in turn search for properties to purchase on the MLS. Most listing services require a real estate license to post. There are many different listing services, and the areas of coverage often overlap. Third-party websites such as zillow.com and trulia.com pull information syndicated by the MLS to display.

There were large amounts of COVID relief money mailed from the US government to US households, which increased their wealth. A desire to move from urban to more rural areas to escape high population densities grew while remote work options increased. It was the perfect storm, and we were in the middle of it.

CHAPTER 10

FEAR OF THE UNKNOWN

COVID brought to light the reminder that "black swan" events can happen, and do happen. Céline started to think about all the investment properties we had acquired up to this point in our portfolio. Having a data-driven method of thought, she concluded that she needed to know certain facts about our real estate portfolio for our future and to plan to retire in our 50s.

At what point should we stop accumulating properties and focus only on paying off the mortgages? Did we have the correct number of properties for the lifestyle we wanted to have in retirement? What would our exact income be from the rent each month?

Black Swan Event: A metaphor coined by Dr. Nassim Taleb in his book *The Black Swan* to describe the occurrences of rare, unforeseen events such as 9/11 attacks, Great Recession, and COVID-19. The historical background of this metaphor is from a widespread belief that black swans did not exist—until they were eventually found in Australia.

Céline did not graduate with a degree in finance like Chris, but understood the importance of financial planning to reach a desired goal. The funds for retirement don't just appear out of nowhere.

She searched high and low for anyone who could help her answer the questions that kept her awake at night. The conclusion was that there is no designated professional who specializes in the area of portfolio planning with real estate assets in the United States for investing—other than real estate securities.

Chris couldn't bear to see her struggle with her fears any longer. He rolled up his sleeves and re-examined the information from his finance degree, real estate licensing, Series 66, and Series 7 licensing. He spent many weeks calculating and creating a multifaceted and extensive report to lovingly answer her unknowns in detail.

This in-depth analysis was a blessing in disguise because we found that we only needed to acquire one more property to reach our personal retirement goals. We were able to find out exactly how much to spend on the next property, how much we needed to charge each month in rent, what type of property to buy, and so much more in detail. We would not have had any idea without the extensive work that Chris did to create the report we now called the *Evans Report for Real Estate Planning*.

What the Evans Report for Real Estate Planning Uncovers for the Investor

- An assessment of goals, desires, risks, and budget
- Long-term and short-term use planning
- Overview of ownership structure and pros and cons
- Target date retirement cash flow planning
- Analysis of existing or hypothetical portfolios given real-world parameters
- Projected cash flow of the existing or hypothetical portfolio
- SWOT (strengths, weaknesses, opportunities, and threats) analysis identifying target markets for investing
- Financial modeling of leverage reduction timelines

- Depreciation projections
- Property type recommendations (commercial, residential, one-to four-unit multi-family, five- or more unit multi-family)

A reasonably priced property available for sale was still rare. Sellers were commanding record prices from buyers at this point in time, and buyers were willing to pay the price and more. Mortgage rates were still in the range of 2% and 3%, keeping borrowed money affordable. There were some home showings that turned entire neighborhood streets into parking lots. Buyers clamored to view a property that had been listed just the day before. There were also multiple bidding wars calling for the highest and best offer to be presented.

We both worked nonstop during this real estate boom. We are real people and soon found ourselves in dire need of some sort of vacation from everyday life. There was an added sense of cabin fever from avoiding society and gatherings due to COVID-19. We wanted to explore the world we live in because life is short.

Céline had traveled to Alaska for a few summers in her early childhood to fish for silver salmon. The trips were remembered fondly. She wanted to share her early experiences with our children, and it wasn't likely that we would contract the coronavirus while fishing outdoors. It was decided that we would go for seven days while taking health precautions on the airplane.

We spent the vacation reminiscing about the fun times she had as a child and soaked up the tranquility of the beautiful state. Naturally, we were curious about real estate because we worked in the industry. We got back to Georgia and realized that we wanted to own property in Alaska too. It brought us so much joy in life.

Meanwhile, the high value of the properties for sale in metro Atlanta did not look sustainable to us. Céline remembers Chris saying in disbelief,

"There's just no way our property is worth this much." We asked ourselves if the metro Atlanta market was overinflated, and if we should exit.

Further research found that Alaska's real estate prices had not inflated as much as Georgia's had. We decided to use the high equity we had in the Georgia market to transfer to the seemingly more stable Alaska market. The transfer had to be done before anything happened to bring Georgia prices down.

We researched the various cities and towns we were most familiar with near Anchorage. Some household income information and personal opinions on neighborhoods were easily found online, but the best advice came from a local real estate agent who was born and raised in Alaska. Yes, we hired an agent when we were real estate agents ourselves. The local knowledge about an area, as well as professional help with the different nuances in Alaska real estate purchase and sale contracts, was invaluable. We weren't about to pretend that we understood every aspect of real estate transactions in another state just because we were licensed in Georgia.

Our Must-Have List for Our Alaska Property

- Well maintained.
- Convenient location.
- Reasonable HOA costs (if there is an HOA).
- Ability to rent the property to a tenant immediately.
- Reasonable property taxes.

We settled on a duplex we found near the city center of a town about 45 minutes from Anchorage. The property was a short distance to convenient stores such as Target, groceries, and other everyday necessities. There was no HOA, which meant that we could rent the property to tenants in the future. The taxes were also quite reasonable.

However, the property belonged to an older, ailing individual who did not maintain the property well. We got estimates from contractors on the cost of renovation while we inspected the property. We calculated that we could still buy the property and renovate it to a habitable condition with the right sales price.

The sales price agreed upon worked out well. The estimated rental price for just one side was enough to cover the entire mortgage on the duplex. It was as if we were buying two properties for the price of one.

So how did we finance this duplex? This was the first time we were not hermit crabbing our way into ownership of an additional property. We were not intending to live in it as a primary residence, so we couldn't. It turned out that we needed even more money for the down payment because we had to get what is called an investor-grade mortgage.

Investor-grade mortgage loan: Mortgage rates vary by risk. Riskier loans require a higher return to offset that risk to the lien holder. Despite the historic stability and relative low volatility within the real estate market as a whole, there is still risk associated with every loan.

From the lender's perspective, they have risks to consider. For instance, what would happen in a scenario where the borrower loses their job? Well, the most likely scenario here would be that the borrower would pay all loans as long as they could. However, if finances become tight, logic would dictate that the borrower would continue to pay for their primary home's mortgage over the mortgage owed on their investment property.

For this reason, mortgages on investment properties are significantly more restrictive. In our experience, we have found them to have a higher interest rate of between 0.75% and 1.5% over the prevailing residential interest rate. Additionally, they have higher down payment requirements. Borrowers may get away with 3.5% to 5% down for a primary purchase and opt for the mortgage insurance premium (MIP) payment each month, but an investor is typically required to pay at least 20% as a down payment. We've found that the best rates often occur when the down payment is

30% or more. Mortgage lenders remove most risk of taking a loss in the event of default with this big a down payment.

We looked at our first home purchase—the townhouse in Athens. It had been a number of years since we bought it, and the housing market had tanked during the Great Recession. The value of the townhouse was finally above our original purchase price in 2008. We had just enough equity for the investor-grade down payment if we sold the townhouse to buy the duplex.

Yes, we hold tight to our philosophy of not selling properties. However, we were essentially replacing our original townhouse in Athens with a safer investment because the rental market was better in Alaska, and we were less vulnerable during tenant turnover when we increased the number of doors from one to two. This was our own version of risk management.

We also learned more about the 1031 Exchange. This proved to be a fantastic tool for us as our real estate portfolio grew, and we no longer used the hermit crabbing method of acquiring additional properties.

1031 Exchange: When you sell a property for a profit, there is a tax that must be paid to the government called capital gains. This is a tax on the gain you receive from owning that property and making money from the sale of it.

Generally speaking, when you sell your primary residence, the government gives you an exclusion on the capital gain. If the occupancy requirements are met this allows the seller to keep up to $250,000 of the profits if taxes are filed as a single person, or up to $500,000 of the profits if taxes are filed as a married couple.

This exclusion does not exist when the property is not a primary residence. If an investment property is sold, then the investor has realized a gain and pays capital gains tax on their profit from the sale.

Sometimes investors need to reallocate their portfolio before they are ready to liquidate. The 1031 Exchange allows an investor the ability to sell an investment property while deferring the tax payment to a later date.

The individual or entity (Exchanger) in a 1031 Exchange must swap the property for a "like-kind" asset. We will leave it up to the 1031 Exchange experts to advise on what type of properties qualify for that definition.

A third party called a Qualified Intermediary (QI) is used to process the 1031 Exchange. The QI intercedes on behalf of the Exchanger for a few tasks. First, they collect the funds after the sale of the first property and hold them until the second property is purchased. This prevents the Exchanger from ever receiving payment from the first property's sale. The other role of the Qualified Intermediary is to prepare tax forms and account for the dates and funds within the transaction for the Exchanger.

In detail, before the first property is sold, it must be identified as a 1031 Exchange. This is done by notifying the QI that the Exchanger intends to sell the property and use the funds as part of a 1031 Exchange. The contract to sell the first property requires an assignment clause that allows the contract to be assigned to the Qualified Intermediary.

Once the property is placed under contract to sell, the contract is then assigned to the QI to complete the first transaction. After the sale, the QI will receive any proceeds from the transaction that would have been due to the Exchanger. Then the seller will have 45 days to identify potential replacement properties for the 1031. By the 45th day, the QI will need a list of potential properties to be delivered.

The Exchanger will then have up to 180 days to complete a purchase on one of the identified properties. The purchasing contract will also have an assignment clause to the QI. When the replacement contract is ready to close, the QI will wire the funds to the attorney or title office to be used in the purchase of the replacement property.

In general, if 100% of the proceeds are used for the purchase, then there is not a taxable event. If 90% of the funds from the first sale are used, then the remaining 10% is called a boot, and the boot would be a taxable event.

We have found that a QI is worth their fee. They will help coach you throughout the exchange process, advise on property types that qualify, and ensure the transaction is completed properly. We like to have the safety of 1031 Exchange professionals do the heavy lifting to protect us from any errors.

The duplex in Alaska.

It took three months during the winter after our 1031 Exchange to completely renovate the duplex to its potential. We put one side of the property on the market for lease and got a qualified, approved tenant within three days of going on the market with a rent enough to cover both sides of the duplex.

We furnished the other side for ourselves as we intended to stay for a few weeks in the summers. We would be saving on hotel lodging and could keep our fishing gear in Alaska permanently. No more lugging long fishing rods onto a commercial flight. We are sure the passengers appreciate the lack of rod tips pointing at their faces as we walk past them to our assigned seats.

We also purchased an ancient but reliable car for little money to keep at the duplex. It made sense to us to buy the car because in just two visits we would have spent the same amount on a rental car. Alaska is notorious for high rates when it comes to rental vehicles.

Our unit was set up so that when we are not there, we could have extra income from short-term rentals if we chose to let guests stay. We used a Lockly digital lock so we could unlock the unit from Georgia. Anything that we made from renting out to short-tern renters was welcome "bonus mailbox money" for us. All the sweat and labor that went into the whole building proved to be well worth it.

Our yearly fishing trips to Alaska now cost us the price of food and gas. The plane tickets were covered by mileage points earned from simply running our real estate brokerage. Our hearts were full even after it took so much effort to get to where we were.

Our current real estate portfolio inventory (2021)

1. Single-family residential home rented to a tenant.
2. Single-family residential home as a primary residence.
3. Single-family residential home rented to a tenant.
4. Commercial office for our real estate brokerage.
5. Duplex rented to tenants purchased 13 years after purchasing our first home and nine years after officially becoming real estate investors with rental properties.

It was early 2022. We continually watched the real estate prices rise during the pandemic housing boom. Eventually, our other properties in Georgia increased so much in value that we wanted to reinvest the equity in those properties too. We refinanced these houses and used the amount for another investor-grade mortgage loan for an additional property in Alaska.

We contacted our agent in Alaska to start the search for our second investment home there. Here is a list of what we looked for when considering the potential homes.

Our Must-Have List for Our Second Alaska Property
- Well maintained.
- Convenient location.
- Reasonable HOA costs (if there is an HOA).
- Ability to rent the property to a tenant immediately.
- Reasonable property taxes.

We located a basic, single-family home in the southern part of Anchorage that fit our needs. The sales price was reasonable, there was no HOA, we could rent the property to a tenant, and the rental market for the area was outstanding.

Chris was also exhausted from managing our properties in Georgia. Property management can eat a significant amount of your time that could be spent elsewhere, although it can save money if you are managing your own properties. Yet we had so many duties that needed our attention at the real estate brokerage in Georgia we owned. Properties in Alaska meant that someone other than Chris would manage the rental properties. He was so happy about this.

We chose to buy the house we found and rented it back to the seller for a few months while they finished up the contract they had with their employer. The house did not need renovations or repairs other than a brand new set of stainless steel appliances.

The second Alaska property leased quickly within two weeks of it going on the rental market. Our cash flow was increased by a large amount, and the property manager was now in charge of the house.

The second rental property we purchased in Alaska.

Our current real estate portfolio inventory (2022)

1. Single-family residential home rented to a tenant.
2. Single-family residential home as a primary residence.
3. Single-family residential home rented to a tenant.
4. Commercial office for our real estate brokerage.
5. Duplex rented to tenants.
6. Single-family residential rented to a tenant purchased 14 years after purchasing our first home and 10 years after officially becoming real estate investors with rental properties.

In the middle of 2022, the real estate market was still red hot from the ongoing housing boom. In fact, the market was so hot that we worried even more about the sustainability of the prices for our Georgia properties.

We looked at the current sales data and determined that it would be best to leave the metro Atlanta market when we could. We thought, why not use the 1031 Exchange to trade an overvalued Georgia house for a better-built and valuable house in Alaska?

We confirmed our ideas with the calculations from the *Evans Report for Real Estate Planning* and began the process of selling the second real estate purchase we had ever made: the single-family home in Acworth, Georgia, that we had turned into a rental.

The rental house quickly sold within three weeks and was paid in cash by the buyer. The tenants who were renting the property even got to stay. It was a memorable transaction for everyone involved. It was now time to find a property to replace the one we had just sold.

Our Must-Have List for Our Third Alaska Property
- Well maintained.
- Convenient location.
- Reasonable HOA costs (if there is an HOA).
- Ability to rent the property to a tenant immediately.
- Reasonable property taxes.

We found out that the duplex right next to the one we already owned was for sale. It was also listed for the right price. If you have ever played the game Monopoly, you understand the value of having two rental properties next to each other in a rental market. We had found our Boardwalk and Park Place.

The second duplex we purchased in Alaska and our third property we owned in the state.

Principles of the Game of Monopoly

There are many principles the board game teaches about real estate investing, but there is one that applies to this specific situation—owning properties in a color group. In our real-life case, this would equate to owning two rental duplexes side by side.

The Monopoly game rule itself states, "If all Title Deed cards in a color group are owned by a player, DOUBLE RENT is charged. The rule applies even if a property in the color group is mortgaged."

We understood that we could command a higher rent if we owned properties side by side. This was an ideal 1031 Exchange for us as the second duplex was better built compared to the Georgia property we had just sold, and it also increased our door count by one. The increase in door count decreased our risk during tenant turnovers.

The duplex rented quickly after the sale just as the other properties had. By the end of 2022, we were in our mid-30s. We owned our primary residence, had six rental doors, and owned a respectable commercial building.

Our current real estate portfolio inventory (2022)

1. Single-family residential home as a primary residence.
2. Single-family residential home rented to a tenant.
3. Commercial office for our real estate brokerage.
4. Duplex rented to tenants.
5. Single-family residential rented to a tenant.
6. Duplex rented to tenants, purchased 14 years after purchasing our first home and 10 years after officially becoming real estate investors with rental properties.

We had reached a net worth where we felt we could comfortably retire starting in our 50s. This is what our self-employed retirement looks like. We will have monthly rental income from all the owned properties to sustain our daily living—also known as "mailbox money."

We called our portfolio achievement Base Camp One, which is a climbing reference to Mount Everest's Camp One, located approximately 40 miles one way from Lukla, Nepal, and sitting at 19,900 feet in altitude. It takes around 11 to 14 days to reach on foot.

Any investing we do after our own Base Camp One would be in excess of what we need during our retirement. We are truly excited to see the view from the mountain when we are done climbing our own financial "Everest." This portfolio would also be something to pass on to our children to promote generational wealth. Pretty nice, right?

Did it matter that the US Federal Reserve increased rates so rapidly with quantitative tightening in the first half of 2022? What about the price correction that happened after the pandemic housing prices shot through the roof? Yes, they mattered, but also, no, they did not for our purposes.

Quantitative tightening: A monetary policy used to shrink the Federal Reserve's balance sheet. The Federal Open Market Committee's rates are increased, which may help to fight inflation. However, higher FOMC rates are often directly correlated with higher consumer lending costs, which are reflected through higher mortgage loan rates.

Quantitative easing: A monetary policy used to expand the Federal Reserve's balance sheet. The FOMC's rates are lowered, which may help to increase money supply in the economy and spur economic growth. Lower FOMC rates are often directly correlated with lower consumer lending costs, which are reflected through lower mortgage loan rates.

We had already established our portfolio with mortgages that we could properly handle (think about the size of those investor-grade 30% down payments we made). The equity we have in our properties helps shield us from having a high risk of default. Underwriting standards since the housing crash of 2008 are also much tighter now.

Further, we do not plan to sell the properties, so volatility in the housing market has less of an impact on what we are doing now, which is slowly paying off what we owe in its entirety.

Our real-life portfolio story proves that even with the natural ups and downs of a real estate market, you can find opportunities to invest as safely as possible if you know what you are doing. After all, our Base Camp One did start with penniless college students stoking a fireplace for warmth through the Great Recession.

CHAPTER 11

FIVE STEPS TO YOUR PORTFOLIO

W e decided to write in detail when we first discussed the idea of sharing
our investment story. It is our hope that real people like us, possibly
with similar beginnings, burdened with student debt, and a household full
of obligations, will find inspiration and guidance from our experiences to
start their own portfolios.

The following five steps are an outline to get started:
1. Create a Plan
2. Build Your Team
3. Determine Your Financials
4. Search High and Low
5. Keep Investing to Reach Your Own Base Camp One

Create a Plan

You could take many paths when you are ready to start investing in real
estate. A quick internet search will have your head spinning with con-
flicting or misleading information on wholesaling, flipping, short-term
rentals, hard money lenders, property managers, tenant nightmare stories
from the trenches, and so much more. It is very confusing.

Furthermore, states can have significant differences in real estate contracts for buying and selling. There are also regulations on what you can do with your properties, depending on where they are located.

It should be a priority to establish an investment plan to match your individual goals and needs when you are looking to acquire properties. Your plan also needs to be re-evaluated periodically as your portfolio grows.

We firmly believe in the power of planning, but we have also seen investors caught in the planning phase for too long while trying to do it all on their own. This is called analysis paralysis. Our *Evans Report for Real Estate Planning* helps real people like us get a jump start and account for overwhelming variables. Our personalized and professional report is available for every state in the US. See the next chapter for contact information.

Build Your Team

Working within the real estate industry, we have been honored to have firsthand insight that few investors have access to. We have learned how these providers work together through the 3,600+ personal, client, and brokerage transactions we have completed.

A few takeaways that we've observed over that time is that communication, competency, and a relationship-oriented approach to sales often lead to a successful transaction and many more thereafter. Competency can be hard to discern at first.

Acquiring properties over time requires a great team working in conjunction with each other. Your job as the investor is to put your winning team together for a successful transaction. Success or failure is ultimately up to your ability to coordinate and manage the team of professionals while keeping everything on schedule.

Let's talk about a few of these roles in depth and the role they have played within our personal transactions. Make sure to review the professional interview guide in our resource section at hshbrands.com/FromTheGroundUp for detailed questions that we ask when choosing a partner.

Lenders: Lenders are not all created equal. We look for excellent communicators who are highly competent at their job and are able to be competitive on rates. We try to have two or three in our rotation at all times since some lenders will specialize in one situation over another. You'll find many types of mortgage lenders such as banks, large multinational loan companies that advertise on TV, and smaller mortgage companies that may be regional or local. Loan officers are the people who work for lenders. They guide the buyer through the loan application process.

Large national lenders are competitive on price, and they usually require each loan officer to be licensed and registered with the Nationwide Mortgage Licensing System (NMLS). Common issues with large lending firms include the loan officer having little access to their underwriting team, which might cause delays in processing due to knowledge gaps. Large firms are also known for needing longer timeframes to process loans. They are less likely to be well versed in local programs such as down payment assistance.

Local and regional lenders may have better efficiency and processing, but might not be priced as competitively as the large lending behemoths and banks. They usually have expert-level knowledge of local programs and buyer resources. The experience with a local firm is dependent on the experience level of the individual loan officer.

Ultimately, we look for someone who answers when we call or returns calls the same day (or next morning if a late call). When we're entering a new market, we ask for recommendations from real estate agents and interview a few potential lenders whom we test and observe over the first couple of weeks in our planning stage. The best to communicate and show that they understand our goals usually get our business.

Real Estate Agents: Where do we begin? We've turned over 150 real estate agents through our firm since taking over in 2015. Some had what it took and others, well, didn't. When we expanded into Alaska, we asked our network to recommend an agent who could help us from 4,000+ miles away. Our first call was great, but after 10 days passed, she had only completed a fraction of the tasks she promised us. We decided to leave her to her other business and learned that recommendations don't always pan out.

We kept searching for homes and stumbled on Larry when we inquired about one of his listings. After chatting with him for a bit, Larry took the initiative to help us solve our problem. Not only did he set us up on a home search, he provided key insight that helped us narrow our search to a few specific areas. He coordinated virtual tours and got information for properties that we showed interest in. He was an advocate on our behalf and always stuck to his word. He earned our trust by being in our corner and helping us to shape our dreams.

Larry also coordinated the title company and our lender to make sure everything stayed on track for a smooth closing. Larry was our resource for almost everything we needed and a reliable resource to set expectations on timelines and costs.

Attorney: As an investor it is important to have relationships with an attorney who can assist you when needed. An attorney can assist with the legal structure of how to take ownership of the properties, assist with contracts where needed, and generally keep you out of trouble. Ours does.

They can also help create partnership and buy/sell agreements when transacting investments with business partners who are not a spouse.

Some states will have an attorney act as the closing agent for real estate transactions while other states use title companies. If you are in a state that uses a title company, having an attorney may require an effort to find one, but if in an attorney state, we can call an attorney that we use for most of our closings. Find one you can work with.

Property Managers: Property managers often require little more than a real estate license for their state, but need much more to be a reliable professional who you can count on when you need them.

After interviewing 12 different property managers in Alaska, we noted that some kept little more than an Excel spreadsheet for record keeping. Others lacked the ability to direct deposit to our accounts or didn't advertise properties outside of their company website. Our PM has been one of our best partners.

Choose them wisely because they are the company that you'll deal with every month indefinitely. Everyone else is on a per-transaction basis. Not only do they need to be good, but you should like them. Otherwise you'll dread every call you get about a leaky water heater or hailstorm or problem tenant.

So what happens if you have to put a team together quickly? Many people stumble into becoming a real estate investor by either finding a great deal, inheriting a home, or making the decision to keep a home when the need to relocate arises. Often this means a team needs to be put together quickly. With additional oversight and management from the investor's role, deals can still be completed successfully.

When in a position of needing to put together a team fast, the best route is to find the best real estate agent first, then ask them for the referrals to the other pros you need. Experienced agents often have their trusted pros, and you will find that the level of service might be slightly higher given a reputation they need to keep with their referring real estate agent.

Certified Public Accountant (the CPA): As your investing portfolio starts to grow, so do the complexities of filing taxes. Having a professional oversee our taxes properly is incredibly important to us. We have seen extreme cases where investors have lost their entire fortunes due to tax errors, so we take as many precautions as we can in this area.

Insurance agent: A professional to have in your corner, preferably one who has experience in real estate. The agent will help educate you on the many different types of policies available and how they interact with each other. Every owner needs to protect themselves and the property itself from risks.

Here are some of the types of insurance you may need:

Homeowners insurance: This insurance policy covers the following risks:
Liability risks or exposure: Legal costs or medical payments from events that occur on the premises.
Building structure: The cost required to rebuild the property from the ground up.
Personal property: The cost to replace common contents of a home. The amount received is usually calculated by the value of the home itself. Most calculations are made considering 50% of the home value or higher.

Keep in mind that your homeowners insurance policy will need to be within a certain price range per month. The price range is set per the lender if financing the purchase. Have your insurance agent and lender get in contact with each other as soon as you consider buying a property to verify.

Umbrella policies: An insurance policy with additional liability coverage beyond standard policies. These policies may help with personal liabilities, injuries, lawsuits, damage to property, and more.

Commercial insurance: Also known as business insurance. This insurance may cover aspects of your business, ownership of the business, and the employees. Commonly covers items such as commercial property, liabilities, and income.

Landlord insurance: Insurance to cover structural damage, liabilities, and loss of income related to rental properties. These policies do not protect items belonging to the tenant(s) nor do they cover routine repairs.

Renters insurance: Insurance for tenants to cover personal belongings and liabilities in a rented dwelling. May also cover expenses related to displacement from the rental.

Life insurance: Life insurance policies are often used to cover all or part of the cost of a mortgage loan in cases of premature death. This way, the other partner will have a property to live in after an untimely death of a spouse or partner.

Mortgage insurance: Also called a mortgage insurance premium. An insurance policy for lenders in case of nonpayment by the borrower. These policies are commonly required for FHA and USDA loans.

A guide for interviewing professionals can be found on our website: hshbrands.com/FromTheGroundUp.

Determine Your Financials

If following our hermit crabbing method with an institutional loan to start your portfolio, we recommend having at least 10% of the purchase price saved up in cash. This money will be needed for the down payment, closing costs, and other expenses that may come up for the property acquisition.

Other than the actual sales price of the property that will be paid over time in monthly installments, many buyers will need to pay a down payment for the loan and part or all of the closing costs. The typical down payment for an owner-occupant 30-year conventional loan is 5% of the purchase price, and closing costs are typically under 3%.

It is a wise decision to not spend all your money on obtaining properties. You will want to leave the remaining 2% of the 10% in cash as a margin for moving expenses, unexpected financial burdens, or property maintenance that may be discovered after closing. Ideally, the goal will be to find a property that matches the criteria for significantly less than your budget can afford.

The next step is to know what financing you qualify for based on your debt-to-income ratio, credit score, and financial well-being. A loan officer will take your application with the details of personal finances, income, and savings. They will run your credit score and analyze your stated assets. They will then tell you the amount of mortgage loan they are willing to lend you.

Banks or Mortgage Lending Companies?
We like to use professional mortgage lending companies over banks. Why? Banks do not always require their mortgage originators to study and maintain their own individual mortgage originating licenses. Their employees can operate under the bank's charter license. On the other hand, professional mortgage lending companies are required to maintain individual mortgage originating licenses.

It is important to have full confidence in the people processing financial files. We personally have had plenty of exposure to a variety of loan officers and the mortgage lending process. Chris has caught three loan officers in direct lies or schemes that could have turned fraudulent if allowed to continue.

There are other types of financing that are not traditional loans. You will find a list and brief definitions of them next.

Private loan: Some people have strong connections or are lucky to have wealthy family members. While the funds may not be given outright, a loan with little to no interest rate is possible. Terms vary and can be unique.

Hard money loan: These loans are usually provided by nontraditional lenders and are often issued to businesses rather than individuals. The lenders may offer less strict financial requirements for applicants and can quickly provide funds for commercial or residential investment purchases. The property itself is used as collateral to be claimed by the lender if the borrower defaults on repayment.

Construction loan: Building a residential or investment property is possible through a construction loan. These loans still require review of your finances and also require the construction plans and timeline. Money for the build is dispersed in installments. Interest is usually the only amount paid by the owner while construction is ongoing. The loan is converted to a permanent mortgage after construction is complete.

Home equity line of credit: The difference in the amount owed on a mortgage and the value of the property is called home equity. Home equity loans will use a portion of the equity as collateral for a loan called a HELOC. These loans are sometimes used to procure investment properties. Remember that the debt-to-income ratio will be calculated with a HELOC as part of your debt if you plan to finance another loan.

Search High and Low
You will need to find properties that match your portfolio needs with financing for which you qualify. This step can be time consuming and difficult if you are not using the *Evans Report for Real Estate Planning* as your guide. There are a multitude of variables to examine in a property and its community when looking to buy. Be sure to have the right real estate agent working with you to help.

Main Property Attributes to Look For
We like to use the general property attributes we showed in previous chapters to identify our own potential portfolio properties. The following

attributes are a more detailed, but not exhaustive list of additional qualities to consider:

- An area with tenants who are likely to stay in the property for multiple years
- An area with high credit scores
- Fewer than 15 minutes to a major highway
- Schools in the top 30% of the surrounding areas
- Several major employers in the area
- Neighborhood income at least 10% higher than the surrounding areas
- Rental marketing times of not more than 30 days
- Demand for growth in the area forecasted for the next five to 10 years

Age and Condition of Major Components

There are even more items to consider when choosing a property to buy. The costs to repair or replace the following major components can quickly add up. They must be taken into account.

- Roof (typically lasts 20 to 30 years)
- HVAC systems (typically last 15 years at minimum)
- Water heaters (typically last 10 to 15 years unless tankless, which can last twice as long)
- Re-plumbing a home due to polybutylene or aging copper pipes with pinhole leaks (polybutylene is a recalled item, and copper piping lasts about 50 years before breaking down with pinhole leaks)
- Re-plumbing drain lines to replace old cast iron or clay drains (typically last up to 50 years)
- Septic system maintenance, repair, or replacement (can last indefinitely if maintained properly)
- Appliances (lifespans vary)

Lead Paint Warning: If a building was built prior to 1978, any property in the US is subject to the EPA's regulations on lead-based paint. You will want to test for the presence of lead during your due diligence period. (Inspection guidelines vary by state. This is for Georgia.) There are strict requirements for tenant-occupied properties with lead paint. Purchasing newer properties minimizes the risk for the owner.

Hopefully, you are able to find a property that matches your criteria. If not, all hope is not lost. Plenty of other properties can still be considered decent investments. These properties may not check all the boxes on the list and have a higher risk associated with them, but this is investing. No investment comes without risk. Be sure to choose with as much caution as possible. Always consult a professional if you need guidance.

Sometimes, certain properties have potential, but need an extensive amount of work. These properties are not considered "turnkey" real estate properties. You can often negotiate a better purchase price on these homes and can save even more money if you are willing to put some elbow grease into needed repairs yourself.

Keep Investing to Reach Your Own Base Camp One

One mistake we have seen real estate investors make is to give up too soon. Most investments that are worth the effort take time. Think about the years between our early purchases. The time between those purchases was considerably longer than our later purchases due to leverage. This is the same reason investing is often compared to a proverbial snowball that accumulates faster as the portfolio becomes larger.

Determine what your own Base Camp One will look like. What is the purpose of your real estate portfolio? What else can you utilize the portfolio for? Are you looking to create Base Camp Two or beyond? What do you want the portfolio to do after you pass away? As previously stated, don't forget to re-evaluate your profile as your life progresses in order to account for changing needs.

Reminders: Never forget to diversify your investments. Keeping all your investments in one category is akin to putting all your eggs into one basket. Explore other avenues such as index funds, bonds, and more. Diversification can help alleviate the strain on your assets in cases of market shifts.

Don't overlook 1031 Exchanges and other avenues rather than straight sales. Governments often have incentives for residential and commercial owners in the form of tax credits, grants, and more. Research the city, county, state, and federal levels of government to find these incentives. Finally, never stop learning to discover what is possible.

So, did we ever move into a house with two sinks in the master bathroom? No, but maybe one day we will.

EVANS REPORT FOR REAL ESTATE PLANNING

C ontact us for more information on creating a custom plan that covers these areas:

- An assessment of goals, desires, risks, and budget
- Long-term and short-term use planning
- Overview of ownership structure and pros and cons
- Target date retirement cash flow planning estimation
- Analysis of existing or hypothetical portfolios given real-world parameters
- Projected cash flow of the existing or hypothetical portfolio
- SWOT (strengths, weaknesses, opportunities, and threats) analysis identifying target markets for investing
- Financial modeling of leverage reduction timelines
- Depreciation projections
- Property type recommendations (commercial, residential, one- to four-unit multi-family, five- or more unit multi-family)

RESOURCES

Visit hshbrands.com/FromTheGroundUp for resources and worksheets on these topics:

Buyers
- How to improve your credit score
- How to pick a mortgage lender
- Budget worksheet
- How to pick a home inspector
- Closing costs worksheet

Sellers
- Pre-marketing checklist
- Marketing checklist
- Capital gains worksheet
- Home showing tips
- Closing costs worksheet

Homeowners
- New owner checklist
- Moving tips
- Home warranties
- Home maintenance checklist

Landlords

- Marketing tips
- New tenant checklist
- Property management tips
- Home maintenance checklist

REFERENCES

Bloomberg article on college degrees, https://www.
bloomberg.com/news/articles/2022-04-18/
is-college-worth-it-most-graduates-work-in-other-fields

Wharton School of the University of Pennsylvania, paper on the causes
of the 2008 housing boom, https://whr.tn/3f7C79R

The Oxford Economic Papers article (2012) on what happened during
the Great Recession in 2008, https://bit.ly/3dvy3ju

Paper on *The Financial Crisis and the Well-Being of Americans* (2012),
https://www.ncbi.nlm.nih.gov/pmc/articles/PMC3290402/

US Department of the Treasury, Troubled Assets Relief Program (TARP), https://home.treasury.gov/data/
troubled-assets-relief-program

US Environmental Protection Agency Superfund Regulations, https://
www.epa.gov/superfund/superfund-regulations

ACKNOWLEDGMENTS

To Victor and Suzanne Higgins, Céline's parents and Chris's in-laws, thank you for the support you gave us while we started our portfolio. It is also the real estate knowledge that was passed down that helped us become who we are. We would not be where we are today without the guidance you have given.

To Ryan Swails, our dear friend turned insurance agent for so many properties, you educated us and clarified information on the different types of insurance policies for this book. You have provided numerous suggestions on how to protect ourselves in order to keep our investments safe. Thank you for being by our side throughout the years. If he can help you, contact Ryan, ryan.swails@countryfinancial.com, (706) 745-8410.

To Chris Hoitink, Esq., with Mozley, Finlayson & Loggins, LLP, for being our trusted closing attorney since 2016. We have depended on your expertise in real estate law for the majority of our portfolio acquisition. You have been there for us through thick and thin, looking over our shoulder to ensure that we did everything right. We have full confidence in what we were doing because of Chris. To contact him: chrishoitink@mfllaw.com.

To Larry Austin, real estate agent in the Anchorage and surrounding areas of Alaska, for your help in acquiring our properties. You made it all possible to own a piece of Alaskan paradise from 4,000+ miles away in Georgia. Your local knowledge of the Alaskan contracts was invaluable.

Anyone looking to buy or sell property in The Last Frontier should get in contact with him: <u>larryofalaska@gmail.com,</u> (907) 440-0218.

Thanks to our beta readers (in alphabetical order), Cheryl Cappelli, Leslie Ebersole, Scott King, Avril Laurendine, Mark Mizelle, Colleen Novotny, and Peter Waldorf. Thank you for the frank comments and suggestions from your first read. These individuals volunteered their time to tell their thoughts on what was interesting, informative, as well as what needed to be added in the work.

Céline's childhood friends, Meg Hammock, Dr. Elica Fung, Chie Cheng, Yoshika Rexroad, and Avril Laurendine, thank you for being steadfast beacons of friendship.

Brandon Esco, our friend from the time we lived in Athens, Georgia. Thank you for the early morning phone calls to catch up and the support you give us through life.

ABOUT THE AUTHORS

D r. Céline H. Higgins Evans and Christopher S. Evans currently live in the metro Atlanta area. They are second-generation co-owners of Sellect Realty, an independently owned real estate brokerage that is veteran-founded, family-owned, and women-owned.

They have been recognized numerous times for their accomplishments and contributions to the real estate industry.

Sellect Realty was the first brokerage in Georgia to join the FORBES Real Estate Council in 2017. The following year, Chris was named one of the featured agents for *Atlanta Agent Magazine's* Who's Who of Atlanta Real Estate. Their brokerage has since been honored by the University of Georgia's Bulldog 100, which is an award given to top companies owned or operated by UGA alumni.

Chris shared their company's success with industry colleagues shortly after he became principal broker. His willingness to collaborate and in-depth knowledge of real estate catapulted him into the public speaking world. This led to a speaking career that started at one of the largest industry conferences in real estate: the Inman Connect Conference. He has since appeared multiple times.

He also started his own podcast with fellow agents Nathan White and Christian Harris. They released over 130 episodes of the *re:Think Real*

Estate Podcast, which received a 4½ star rating on Apple podcasts. Chris has also been a regular guest on Atlanta Business Radio. He is a two-time featured guest on the *Think Realty* podcast, which is a widely aired show aimed at providing information to the investor side of the industry.

In 2017, Chris began volunteering his time with the Cobb County Association of REALTORS®. This association is the second largest association of REALTORS® in the State of Georgia. He chaired the Real Estate Political Action Committee (RPAC) and is a three-time Education Committee chair alum. He served multiple times on the Strategic Planning Committee and has hosted statewide educational webinars that helped fellow Georgia REALTORS® navigate the pandemic in 2020. He was also awarded the Cobb Association of REALTORS® President's Award that year. He has served as a director to the state and, at the time of this writing, is serving his second two-year term on the board of directors.

Chris and Celine in Alaska.

Céline is an associate broker who personally oversees departments that have turned over more than $44 million annually in sales. She is consistently named in the top 1% of agents across the state based on production volume every year.

The couple have three lovely (most of the time) children—James, Scarlett, and Amélie Clare. The family travels to Alaska for the salmon run each summer. Their favorite places to visit in Alaska are the abandoned Independence Gold Mine and surrounding views of Hatcher Pass, the Kenai River that flows along the city of Soldotna, and the many waterways along the George Parks Highway leading to Denali.

Céline has diverse personal interests. She likes to hand-engrave bird hunting shotguns and Western revolvers, compete for blue ribbons in quilting and canning at the North Georgia State Fair, volunteers her time as a board member with the Fielding Lewis Chapter of the Daughters of the American Revolution, and is constantly entertained by her rescue macaw named Tippet.

Chris loves to tie flies and is a voracious business book reader. He likes to be outdoors, especially to hunt for deer, turkey, and any variety of duck. He can often be found around the house working on small renovation projects or watching *Bloomberg News* for the newest and latest information on markets that affect the real estate industry.

If you are interested in a *Evans Report for Real Estate Planning*, speaking engagements, or real estate sales (residential or commercial), contact us:

Email: info@hshbrands.com
Phone: (770) 509-0265
Website: hshbrands.com

BUILD WEALTH
WITH REAL ESTATE

———

Is real estate part of your investment portfolio? Why not? Real estate is one of the strongest assets to create wealth.

The authors grew their multimillion-dollar real estate portfolio by starting as penniless yet frugally savvy college kids because they figured out how to use leverage and common financial tools to grow their real estate assets.

Chris and Céline walk you through their winning strategy so you can get started on your own real estate portfolio—even if you don't have money, assets, or a plan.

Dr. Céline H. Higgins Evans is an associate broker and co-owner of Sellect Realty. She is consistently named among the top real estate agents in Georgia every year. She holds a degree in biology and veterinary medicine from the University of Georgia.

Christopher S. Evans is an award-winning real estate broker, speaker, and former financial advisor. Chris uses his career experiences, degree in finance from the University of Georgia, and expertise as a principal broker to create custom real estate portfolio investment plans.

www.ingramcontent.com/pod-product-compliance
Lightning Source LLC
Chambersburg PA
CBHW071434210326
41597CB00020B/3780